EVERYTHING YOU WANT
TO KNOW ABOUT
THE LIVING LEGEND,
BO JACKSON

"In 35 years, I've never seen a player with that kind of athletic ability come into [baseball]. . . . we're talking about one of the finest athletes of our time."
—Al Stewart, Scouting Director, Kansas City Royals

"Everyone I talk to says the same thing—he's the best runner they have ever seen."
—Howie Long, All-Pro Defensive End,
Los Angeles Raiders

"He is one of those rare ones that comes along only so often. . . . he will go down as one of the legends of the game."
—Sam Wyche, Coach, Cincinnati Bengals

"I don't care if I go 2-for-200, I'm going to have confidence. I'm the type guy that won't let you beat me."
—BO JACKSON

St. Martin's Paperbacks by
Stephen Hanks

WAYNE GRETZKY
BO JACKSON

HOW TO WIN AT NINTENDO® GAMES

Jeff Rovin

The Nintendo videogame system is the ultimate in home entertainment—an unrivaled source of excitement and challenge. And *How to Win at Nintendo Games* can help you get to the top of your form! Now packed with more vital information than ever, the new updated and expanded edition of *How to Win at Nintendo Games* covers all of your favorite games!

How to Win at Nintendo Games is an unofficial guide—not endorsed by Nintendo®. Nintendo is a registered trademark of Nintendo of America Inc.

BO JACKSON

Stephen Hanks

A 2M COMMUNICATIONS LTD.
PRODUCTION

ST. MARTIN'S PAPERBACKS

BO JACKSON

Copyright © 1990 by Stephen Hanks and 2M Communications Ltd.

Photo research by Amanda Rubin.
Cover photograph (football) by Scott Cunningham, NFL Photos; (baseball) by Tom DiPace, Focus on Sports.

ISBN: 0-312-92394-5

Printed in the United States of America

St. Martin's Paperbacks edition/September 1990

10 9 8 7 6 5 4 3 2 1

Acknowledgements

Many thanks to television station Channel 6 in Birmingham, Alabama, the Birmingham Library's Southern History Department, and to the media relations departments of the Kansas City Royals, Los Angeles Raiders, and Auburn University. Special thanks to Beatrice Hanks, who as a wife and business partner is one of the great two-sport athletes; to multi-sport expert and research whiz Jim Morganthaler; and to my friend Steve Bloom, who can write about basketball and jazz simultaneously, and who should have been mentioned in my earlier Wayne Gretzky book.

To my baseball idol Tom Seaver, and my football hero Joe Namath, who gave me moments of joy, pleasure, and exhilaration that I will never forget.

Bo
Knows
Greatness

If anybody wanted living proof that evolution is one of the soundest scientific theories in the history of mankind, all he would have to do is study an athlete named Bo Jackson.

If anybody wanted to see an athlete who defines that tired sports cliché—"He can do it all!"—all he would have to do is watch Bo Jackson.

If anybody wanted to silence one of those "athletes were better in my day" debates, all he would have to do is mention the name Bo Jackson.

And if anybody wanted to know who the greatest athlete of his time is, all he would have to do is listen to one of his peers talk about Bo Jackson.

Baseball star Mark McGwire: "Bo is God."

Bo Jackson may not be godlike, but as *Newsweek* magazine proposed in December 1989, he may be the best athlete in America. Which in this culture, come to think of it, makes him about as godlike as one can get. But what makes Bo Jackson even more of a national treasure than, say, basketball superstar Michael Jordan, is that by the age of twenty-seven, Jackson had become a superstar in *two* professional sports. Nobody but Bo Jackson can hit a 95-

mile-per-hour major-league fastball 500 feet, and a few weeks later run through an NFL defense for a 90-yard touchdown. As the great heavyweight boxer Mike Tyson put it in *Newsweek:* "You have to respect anybody who can fly like Jordan, but I love the fact that Bo can do *everything.*"

And even Jordan admitted: "If you want to compete with Bo Jackson, somewhere along the line you better prove your versatility."

In his third full season as an outfielder for the Kansas City Royals in 1989, Bo Jackson hit 32 home runs, drove in 105 runs, and stole 26 bases. And his spectacular first-inning home run made him the Most Valuable Player in the annual mid-season All-Star Game. After a two-week rest at the end of the baseball season, Bo began his third year as a fullback for the Los Angeles Raiders, playing the sport he once referred to as his "hobby." In 11 games, Bo ran for 950 yards, the sixth highest total in the American Football Conference. (Projected over a 16-game NFL schedule, Bo's yardage total would have been 1,350, second in the conference.) His 5.5 yards-per-carry average was second in the AFC, and his 92-yard run against the Cincinnati Bengals made him the first player in NFL history to run for 2 touchdowns of 90 yards or more in a career (the other was a 91-yarder against the Seattle Seahawks in a famous 1987 Monday-nighter). Is it any wonder that United Press International named Bo Jackson 1989's "Athlete of the Year" and *Sport* magazine called him "the Most Exciting Athlete in the World"? Bo Jackson's level of excellence in two pro sports is a feat unparalleled in American sports history.

Not that there haven't been some notable two-sport professional athletes. During the 19-teens Jim Thorpe and George Halas, two of America's sports immortals, played both football and baseball, though neither distinguished himself as a star in baseball. In the 1960s, Dave De-Busschere was an NBA basketball player and a pitcher for the Chicago White Sox. But after two mediocre seasons on the mound, DeBusschere devoted himself exclusively to hoops and became an all-star. Veteran New York Yankee outfielder Dave Winfield has never played another sport professionally, but he was such a great athlete in college that a pro football team drafted him even though he never played the sport at the University of Minnesota. And the Los Angeles Dodgers' 1988 World Series hero Kirk Gibson was once an All-American wide receiver and baseball player for Michigan State. Gibson probably could have played both sports as a pro, but has admitted that baseball is such a difficult game that it is nearly impossible to play football at the same time.

Not until Bo Jackson came along had an athlete been able to distinguish himself in pro baseball and pro football simultaneously. So when arguing about human evolution and the merits of today's athletes versus those of yesteryear, one should consider these facts:

In a 1989 book called *The Football Abstract*, authors Bob Carroll, Pete Palmer, and John Thorn note that since 1920, not one of the 23 men before Jackson who played pro baseball and pro football in the same year could do it for more than two seasons, and nobody had done it at all since Vic Janowicz in 1954. (Janowicz is the only other Heisman Trophy winner besides Jackson to play major-league baseball. In 1989, Deion Sanders became the twenty-fifth baseball-football player. He played briefly that summer in the outfield for the New York Yankees, then played defensive back for the Atlanta Falcons.)

By the end of a baseball season—with its relentless schedule and coast-to-coast travel—most players welcome their three- to four-month respite. Bo Jackson, on the other hand, takes a quick breather and proceeds to play one of the most punishing positions in professional sports at an all-pro level. But Bo Jackson's two-sport accomplishment is even more remarkable when one considers how much pressure he's been under to prove himself as a baseball player. Few so-called "experts" thought he made the right decision in 1986 when he chose baseball over football after winning the coveted Heisman Trophy in 1985 as a senior running back at Auburn University. While Jackson had always been an impressive baseball player (the New York Yankees had drafted him in the second round after he finished high school), his innate diamond skills were unpolished compared with the extraordinary natural gifts he displayed as a running back. Fans, sportswriters, even fellow athletes wondered how Jackson could pass up instant stardom in pro football for the years of minor-league training necessary to master the varied and subtle skills of an adequate baseball outfielder, let alone an All-Star.

The answers were obvious to the people who really knew Bo. Football had always been his third-favorite sport (behind track and baseball), and even if his football salary surpassed what he could earn initially from baseball, the threat of a career-ending injury was much more ominous in football. But those same sports observers were even more incredulous when, in 1987, during his first full year with the Kansas City Royals, Bo decided he would play pro football with the Los Angeles Raiders once the baseball season ended. "How could Jackson ever improve at baseball," they asked, "if he didn't concentrate on it year-round? And who is this guy to call football a 'hobby,' anyway? He hasn't proved anything yet."

The coverage of Bo Jackson's two-sport odyssey has not been one of media's better moments. Instead of celebrating Jackson's extraordinarily difficult quest, they ridiculed his decisions and only grudgingly recognized what was becoming an incomparable achievement. Would the predominantly white sporting press have reacted the same way had Bo Jackson not been a black man? If Larry Bird or Joe Montana or Wayne Gretzky wanted to play baseball in their off-seasons, would the media have criticized their decisions? To Bo's credit, he never made race an issue. He just absorbed the written and verbal blasts and went about proving them wrong.

The popular commercials in which he now appears for Nike athletic shoes may joke about what sports "Bo knows," but as Jackson's critics quickly found out, if there is anything that Bo knows, it's his own capabilities and what he wants to do with his life. "I don't think you should put limits on people and what they can accomplish," Bo declared publicly. During the fall of 1989, he appeared on "The Arsenio Hall Show" and said, "The critics out there who think Bo should do this and Bo should do that . . . to make a long story short, they can go to hell." When in 1989 Bo began excelling at baseball and football and other sports on TV spots, he showed people what happens when anyone doubts Bo Jackson's ability.

Tampa Tribune sports editor Tom McEwen was one of many writers who called Jackson "selfish" when he announced his deal with the Raiders in the summer of '87. But after Bo's MVP performance in the '89 All-Star Game, McEwen was singing a different tune. "Many of those people who thought Bo couldn't play baseball and football at the same time or thought he chose wrongly are having second thoughts now. And I'm one of them. I admire him."

"I didn't think he could play both sports," admitted Bo's teammate, Willie Wilson, Kansas City's veteran center fielder. "But I went up to him [during the '89 season] and told him I was sorry because he *can* do both."

One of the best perspectives of Bo and the two-sport argument was offered by Los Angeles Raiders running-back coach, Joe Scannella. "Hey, times have changed," Scannella told *Sport* magazine. "Our society is different. We all want to do what he's doing. Young people understand this. That's why they like him so much. They see a guy doing what he wants to do, not what other people tell him to do. If we could, we would all do it. I think we try to make him more than he is, some kind of mystical guy. Do you want to know what he really is? He's just a regular guy playing two sports."

Vincent Edward Jackson's nickname, "Bo," is short for "boar hog," which is what he was—mean and wild and strong—while he was growing up as a burly bully in the Birmingham, Alabama, suburb of Bessemer. "Bo" could now just as easily be short for "bodacious," an adjective that is synonymous with "noteworthy," or "having a quality that attracts one's attention." But that definition doesn't adequately describe Bo Jackson because he doesn't just *attract* folks with his ability, he hits people over the head with it.

Jackson's talent is not that of Michael Jordan's gravity-defying body contortions, fellow basketball star Magic Johnson's stylish versatility, hockey star Wayne Gretzky's subtle instinctiveness, or the great quarterback Joe Montana's poise-and-precision leadership. Jackson's talent is a blend of two potent ingredients—speed and strength. Such innate assets allow Bo to make any athletic movement seem second nature, even with limited training. With cannon-balls for biceps and battering rams for thighs, Jackson's athleticism is not elegance in motion. Rather, every move made by this six-foot-one, 222-pound mass of muscle (amazingly, he's hardly ever lifted weights to mold his Adonis-like body) is an expression of sheer power. As a baseball hitter, the velocity he generates on his swing joins forces with his strength to produce home runs of unequaled distances. As a football running back, it's his subtle ability to accelerate instantly, as well as his strength, that makes him an elusive and feared ball carrier. Speed, strength, velocity, acceleration, power. Watching Bo Jackson is watching physics at work.

But Bo's former Auburn football coach, Pat Dye, suggests Jackson's special brand of greatness stems from more than just physical skills. Dye feels Jackson possesses a genius that can't be analyzed. "I'm not saying he's great in science or math, although maybe he could be," Dye explained to *GQ [Gentleman's Quarterly]* magazine for a Bo Jackson cover story in April of 1990. "But what separates Bo from other athletes is how smart he is. I never had a player at Auburn with the retention he had. Put it on the blackboard and he'd go do it. Or if he did it a month ago, he'd come back and do it again. You don't step out of baseball, practice football after just two days and then line up to play without [having] a brilliant mind. You can't be an average ol' dumb-ass and do that."

While Bo Jackson hasn't yet led his team to pro championships, as have Magic, Montana, and Gretzky, or dominated his sport during any one season like Jordan, he has already performed the kind of single athletic feats, especially on a baseball field, that are mythic, even by the standards of major-leaguers. One of those rare players even his peers watch take batting practice, Bo Jackson has become a combination comic-book hero/folk legend. He's part Superman, part Incredible Hulk, part Paul Bunyan, part John Henry. And, to paraphrase the song about that steel-drivin' man, oh, how Bo Jackson can hammer a baseball, how he can run, how he can throw! Just listen to the folktales that are quickly becoming legendary.

Hitting: During a game against the Baltimore Orioles in 1988, Jackson stepped out of the batter's box and asked the umpire for time out as pitcher Jeff Ballard went into his windup. The umpire didn't grant time and Bo jumped back into the box as the ball was thrown. Jackson swung and the ball ended up over the center-field fence.

During a spring training game against the Boston Red Sox in 1989, Jackson hit a 515-foot homer over a 71-foot scoreboard. "He hits the ball harder than anybody I've ever seen," said one player. "He can swing late, not hit the ball good, and it still goes over four hundred feet."

During batting practice before a game against the Minnesota Twins at the Metrodome, Jackson hit a majestic fly ball that soared past the dome lights and hit a sign on the facade of the second deck in right center field. One writer described it as "like the last scene in *The Natural.*" The blast was estimated to be 450 feet, just 30 feet short of the longest ever hit to right field in the Metrodome. And Bo, a righty, had hit it batting left-handed.

Running: During a game against the Twins, Bo was caught off third on a missed squeeze play. The shortstop ran toward Bo to start a rundown between third and home. Jackson simply beat the throw to the plate.

Early during the '89 season, Twins scout Jerry Terrell was sitting in the stands rating the Royals players. Jackson hit a ground ball to shortstop and, as all scouts do, Terrell clicked his stopwatch to time Bo down the first-base line. When Terrell looked at the time on his watch, he became annoyed. "Ah, I didn't get him," he said to some fellow scouts. "I must have clicked too soon. His time is too fast." When one of the other scouts asked Terrell what he had, he told him, "Three-point-six-one seconds." The other scouts had the same time. "Four flat is fast from the left side. Three-six-one from the right side, and not on a bunt, is unheard of."

"I've seen him running bases," said Bo's Kansas City teammate Pat Tabler, "freeze halfway between third and home, then be back at full speed in one step. I've seen him hit a two-hopper to short and turn it into a base hit."

"Look, you want to know how fast Bo Jackson is?" a major-league scout told a *Washington Post* sportswriter. "I saw him hit a ball to deep center field. He ran out and caught it, then turned around and beat his own throw back to the plate."

Despite these superhuman feats, including diving catches after outfield dashes and 300-foot heaves from the outfield to home plate on a fly, Bo isn't a completely polished baseball player. He's still making up for all those days spent running track and playing football at Auburn, the lack of time he had to study the baseball craft in the minor leagues, and his admittedly poor work habits as a Royals rookie. Bo still misjudges fly balls, overthrows cutoff men, and can be a very undisciplined batter, but even when he fails he does it with a flourish.

"I saw him break a bat in Detroit once," recalled Tigers coach Alex Grammas, "and the big end flew all the way into the upper deck." But some of Bo's bat shatterings aren't accidental. Jackson still has a propensity for striking out (he averaged 150 K's between '87 and '89), and after particularly frustrating whiffs, Bo will bust his bat into two pieces over various body parts. Such antics compelled a Kansas City television station to produce a promotional ditty sung to the tune of Simon and Garfunkel's "Cecilia":

> Oh, Bo Jackson, you're breaking your bat,
> You're breaking your hat with the timber,

Oh, Bo Jackson, you're all that we've got
We're winning a lot so be cool—
Just be cool . . .

Even watching Jackson's mistakes can be worth the price of admission to a game. Toronto Blue Jays scout Gordon Lakey recalled a 1989 play Bo made at Royals Stadium that had him shaking his head in amazement. "He went to the wall to grab a home run, and he was waiting with his glove over the fence. The ball died and landed at his feet, so that made him look bad. But I'll tell you, that was an unbelievable play. That wall is twelve feet high, and if that ball had been in the first couple rows, he would have caught it."

But as Bo Jackson gains experience, his baseball blunders will disappear.

"Even with the mistakes," Lakey said, "he has an unbelievable impact on every game he's in."

And as Royals manager John Wathan has said, "The more he plays, the better he gets. And I don't have any idea when that will stop."

One hears the accolades of other sports folks and one realizes that, like Jordan, Magic, Montana, and Gretzky, Bo Jackson is becoming an athlete for the ages.

"The guy's more than just some freak show," said an American League scout. "He's just in his own category."

"Bo is not just anybody," raved Royals teammate and future Hall of Famer George Brett, "He's a superhuman."

"What he is," said San Diego Padres general manager Jack McKeon, "is the best damn free-agent signing in the history of the game."

"I always watch him," American League superstar Kirby Puckett of the Minnesota Twins admitted. "An athlete like that comes along every—what would you say?—twenty-five years."

"I can't wait to tell my grandkids one day that I played with Bo Jackson," said Royals teammate Frank White.

But in 1989, two sports writers probably put Bo's talent in the best perspective yet. *Los Angeles Times* football writer Mark Heisler compared Jackson to Jimmy Brown, considered the greatest power back in NFL history. Heisler observed that unlike the talented defensive players Jackson was up against, "Brown played against a bunch of white guys who couldn't catch him and wouldn't have known what to do with him if they had."

And in a *Sports Illustrated* cover story on Bo, baseball writer Peter Gammons wrote: "No longer does one have to say 'Bo Jackson' any more than one had to add 'Ruth' to the Babe or 'Presley' to Elvis. Bo, in just his third full season, has reached single-name stature."

And does Bo Jackson, who has traveled from a childhood of fighting and family struggles to an adulthood of fame and fortune (by the end of 1990, his combined earnings from baseball, football, and endorsements should put him in the pleasant neighborhood of about $4 million per year), share those opinions about his greatness? Has the man with a habit for referring to himself in the third person become the proverbial "legend in his own mind"?

"Whether I'm great or not is not for me to say. That's not for Bo to say. I've been playing baseball and football since I was a teenager, and I don't see Bo as a great player. Great players are ones who performed in the past."

If those athletes enshrined in Halls of Fame are the "great players" Bo is talking about, then people will have to come up with another adjective to describe Vincent Edward Jackson. Because a couple of decades from now Bo may have plaques in *two* sports museums.

Bo
Knows
Trouble

In the spring of 1984, Bo Jackson was a twenty-one-year-old with a future that was the envy of millions of American kids. After two superb seasons as a running back for Auburn University, he was the favorite for the Heisman Trophy and a good bet to sign a seven-figure pro-football contract after the '85 season. But on one particular spring day, Bo was less interested in talking about his future than about his past.

Bo had driven through some cyclone-ravaged towns in Alabama to appear at the state's Institute for the Deaf and Blind. He had been invited by the students at the Helen Keller School, and the local high school and college hero was only too happy to oblige. Bo genuinely loved kids, so much so that he was majoring in child development at Auburn. Jackson was so comfortable around those children that the speech impediment he had difficulty controlling around adults was barely noticeable. As Bo began to speak in his soft, measured tones, the kids gazed intently at the interpreter who was relaying his message in sign language.

"All I want to say to you," Bo began, "is don't run life

too fast. You only have one. You'll either be somewhere serving time or pushing up daisies. Obey your parents. In my life there've been three roads: a high road, a low road, and, in between, a just road. Right now I'm on that just road. With God's help, I'm just about to get to the top, to the high road.''

Bo Jackson urged the kids to steer away from the low road, to drive right past trouble. And if there was anyone in Alabama who was an expert on childhood trouble it was Bo Jackson. It seemed as if Bo and mischief had been joined at the hip since the day Bo was born on November 30, 1962.

His mother named him Vincent Edward, after the actor Vince Edwards, the star of her favorite television show, ''Ben Casey.'' Unfortunately, Vincent Jackson (the surname came from his maternal grandparents) was not born into a family like those seen on TV shows of the '60s. He was the eighth of ten children born to Mrs. Florence Bond, who wasn't married to Bo's father, a Bessemer steelworker. Florence worked 12- to 16-hour days as a motel cleaning woman so the fatherless family could squeeze into a small, three-room house. As Bo once recalled, ''We slept wherever we could find a vacant spot.'' Because he didn't always have a blanket to put over him, Bo would often sleep next to the little gas heater in the living room. ''But I knew,'' Bo added, ''that my mom would take care of me.''

Florence Bond must have been a very strong woman. Not only did she manage to support ten children (five boys and five girls), but she had to tame her Vincent, a child who was so strong and wild that the family called him a ''boar hog,'' after the kind of pig that terrorized other animals. The nickname ''Bo'' came from abbreviating ''boar hog'' to ''bo'hog.'' And ''Bo'hog'' was a terror, all right. If he lacked attention at home, he'd get it outside by being the neighborhood bully. By the age of eight, the powerful Bo could take the hardest licks to the stomach his brothers could dish out, and he could beat up kids three to five years older than he was. He would break windows and steal candy bars and, just for fun, would pay kids to beat up other kids. He'd steal money from his mother and take lunch money from schoolmates and lend it back to them—with interest. He once hit one of his cousins with a baseball bat just because she took away a Ping-Pong paddle from him. There was one guy in the neighborhood he'd hit in the head every week as if it were a ritual. And if he couldn't intimidate a guy, he could outrun him. Bo liked hurting people and liked his reputation as the local troublemaker. As his mother would later recall, "You just didn't dare Bo."

"I was buck-wild in those days," Bo admitted. "I did my share of being bad. There was always violence, whether I was beating somebody up or somebody was beating me up—you always had to take care of yourself. Being the eighth of ten kids, I was always into it with my older brothers and sisters. And every time someone in the neighborhood got beat up or hit in the head with a rock or got a bike stolen or there was a broken window, they'd come looking for me."

One time they came looking for Bo and he almost ended up where his mother once predicted he might be before he reached his twenty-first birthday—in the state penitentiary.

It happened in the summer of 1976, when Bo was thirteen and the leader of a gang of about 20 teen-aged boys. Several days after Bo and his friends had terrorized some pigs by throwing rocks into a pen from a steep neighborhood hill, they returned to the pen with the idea of splattering some serious swine. Bo and the boys grabbed rocks and baseball bats and, squealing with delight, went on a rampage through the pen. Blood gushed from the battered heads of pulverized pork, and the pigpen was quickly transformed into a hog cemetery. As sticks and stones continued to be hurled at the animal carcasses, a gun went off. The swift Bo was the first out of the pen. He raced home and changed out of his bloody clothes, but he hadn't been fast enough. The man who fired the shot, a Baptist minister who owned the hog pen, had seen Bo and was soon at Florence's front door, telling Bo's mother that her son was responsible for the death of $3,000 worth of pigs.

As far as Florence was concerned, that was the last straw. Nothing had worked with the hoodlum she had for a son: not the talks or the punishments or the visits to church. She told the minister that if he wanted to have Bo sent to reform school, she wouldn't stand in the way. Bo suddenly became frightened. He remembered an escapade before the pig-killing incident that could have landed him in jail. Bo had jumped a kid from the ninth grade. Obviously not impressed by Bo's reputation for beating up on older kids, the ninth-grader popped Bo in the nose twice and knocked him cold. That was something that Bo, who had never lost a fight, could not let go unpunished.

"The next day," Bo recalled in *Life* magazine, "I got my brother's twenty-two-caliber rifle and waited for him in the field. I had him in my sights, with the gun up to my shoulder. Then I began to remember the things my brother told me about being in reform school—how he didn't sleep for two weeks and how some guys tried to rape him. Stuff like that. I took the shells out of the gun and went home."

So the minister who saw Bo kill the pigs was giving the kid another chance to escape reform school. Lucky for Bo that the pen didn't belong to the local sheriff. The minister told Bo he wouldn't call the police if Bo and his friends agreed to pay for the damage they had inflicted. So for the next six months, Bo and his gang worked mornings and nights, before and after school, at whatever jobs they could find, and eventually paid off the $3,000 debt.

While he ran errands and performed odd jobs for people in his neighborhood, Bo had plenty of time to think about the direction in which his life was going. He thought about how he wanted no part of the drug scene that some of his gang friends were involved in. He'd once found a marijuana cigarette in a paper bag at school, and when he got home he smoked it in a locked bathroom with the window open. He got so high that he ate almost everything in the refrigerator and was sick for two days. No more drugs for Bo, ever, he decided.

Bo also thought about how he liked the feeling of responsibility in earning money. He thought about how hard his mother worked to keep him clothed and fed, and about how much he loved his family. He thought about his mother's Christian beliefs and how he was ready to let the Lord into his life. ("At that point," he told *Ebony* magazine in 1988, "I wanted to be a Baptist preacher, but the Big Man upstairs had something else for me to do.") He thought about his brothers and sisters, many of whom had barely graduated high school. And he thought about whether he could be the first of Florence's children to get a college education.

But he knew his mother would never be able to afford one year's college tuition, let alone four. If Bo was going to be a college graduate one day, he knew that his best chance for a diploma was through a sports scholarship. And if there was one thing young Bo Jackson knew besides how to get into trouble, it was how to handle himself on an athletic field.

Bo
Knows
Sports

Nobody would have blamed the good folks of Bessemer for believing that young Vincent Jackson would never amount to anything in life. Not in their wildest imaginings could they think that the wild, neighborhood kid who killed pigs, stole money, and bashed heads would someday be honored as a local hero. But today, when one drives past the athletic field of McAdory High School in McCalla, Alabama, one sees a sign that reads: HOME OF BO JACKSON. Funny thing is, that sign would probably have been erected even if Bo Jackson hadn't gone on to achieve fame in college and professional sports. He became an Alabama legend simply by virtue of his athletic exploits at McAdory High.

Sports had always come easily to Bo. The running and jumping in track and the throwing of a baseball were just extensions of the skills he crafted for his role as the neighborhood bully. As a child, he was big for his age and possessed the kind of lithe, muscular body that enabled him to compete with older kids. As a third-grader, he made the elementary school track team when he beat fourth-, fifth-, and sixth-graders in a 60-yard dash. Third-graders had not been allowed on the team, but after watching Bo in action, the school principal—who was also the track coach—wisely waived the rule.

When Bo was eleven, his mother urged him to join the local Little League, hoping baseball would keep her son out of trouble. Bo still caused problems, only this time it was for the other players. After years of throwing heavy rocks at anything that moved, Bo had developed a pretty good arm. And compared to those mini-boulders, a baseball must have felt like a bee-bee to Bo. When the Little League coaches saw Bo buzz balls by the temples of terrified tots, they put him in a league for older boys. Even though he hated pitching because "it was too boring. You just stand there and throw the ball," he was soon hurling fast balls past 15-year-olds. "After that," Bo recalled, "I was playing in a men's semi-pro league, even though I was supposed to be in a Pony League."

Bo may have been younger than the athletes he competed against, but, almost sixteen, he was older than most of his freshman high-school class at McAdory in 1978. His age, size (he was about five-foot-ten, 160 pounds then), and obvious toughness earned Bo respect among the classmates and friends he'd made at the school since the seventh grade. These kids were nothing like the drugged-out gang he could have fallen in with in Bessemer. Impressed by Bo's athletic body, his speed, and the tales of his Little League exploits, fellow students and the school's coaches urged him to try out for McAdory's junior varsity football team. Against the objections of his mom, who didn't want him injured playing such a rough sport, Bo attended a tryout scrimmage. Coach Dick Atchison was amazed at all the things Bo could do, like run from sideline to sideline and tackle a ball carrier from behind. Bo's aptitude for football was even more amazing, considering Jackson had never played the sport in his young life.

"That was my first memory of Bo," Atchison recalled, "and even though he wasn't an outstanding football player right away, you could tell he was gonna be something. He was just a big, fine-lookin' young'un. He really caught our eye when he came out for track that spring. He was doing things in the ninth grade that seniors couldn't do." Like finishing tenth in a 60-field decathlon meet despite never having thrown the shot, hurled the discus, or pole-vaulted. And when he wasn't running track, he was playing the outfield and pitching on the baseball team.

His love for running around a track, his ability to smack baseballs long distances, and his affinity for zigzagging around a football field made Bo follow the straight and narrow as a McAdory student. He passed his classes and didn't succumb to the peer pressure of his drugged-out old friends because the gang from Bessemer weren't Bo's peers anymore. "My mother and my high-school coaches helped turn me around from the troublemaking kid I was," Jackson once admitted. Bo was no longer a kid of the streets. He wanted to make something of himself, and by the time his freshman year had ended he knew sports would be his ticket to college and success.

When Bo returned to McAdory for his sophomore year, he was still a teenager but looked like a grown man. Over the summer his height had increased to six feet and he was about 170 pounds of solid muscle. Such growth was remarkable since Bo's most strenuous activity that summer, besides some pickup baseball and basketball, had been casting a fishing line off the bank of a neighborhood pond. When Dick Atchison saw the new, improved Bo, who was not only bigger, but faster, he decided to make him a running back as well as a defensive lineman. Although Bo didn't assume a big load of the running until late in the season, he still gained 400 yards, almost as many gained by the other McAdory runners for the entire schedule. In his junior year, Bo's yardage output increased to 800 yards. And as the team's number-one runner in his senior year, he was All-State, with a whopping 1,173 yards (on 108 carries) and 17 touchdowns. During Jackson's three seasons on the varsity football team, McAdory won 27 of 31 games.

"He kept getting bigger, stronger, and faster every year," Coach Atchison recalls about Bo, who, by his senior year, was six-foot-one and 205 pounds. "And he probably would have gained a lot more yardage had we not played him so much. Sometimes he'd run only ten, eleven times a game, because he was playing defense, punting, kicking field goals, returning kicks, and blocking for our two other backs. Bo was a great blocker. I think the best play I ever remember him making had nothing to do with running. It was blocking. We were playing for the county championship Bo's senior year and on this one play he threw three consecutive incredible blocks to spring another runner for a sixty-five-yard touchdown.

"And, of course, he would do other amazing things," continued Atchison. "There's so many, you can't remember them all. Another one I do recall is a defensive play where he sacked a quarterback just after the guy had thrown the ball. Bo got up, ran toward the receiver about ten yards away, and tackled him from behind. The only guy who can do that is [New York Giants] Lawrence Taylor."

But while Bo saw football as a means to an end, as a vehicle that could get him into college, track was his first love. "Bo tolerated football," McAdory baseball coach

Terry Brasseale revealed. "He didn't really like football until midway through his senior year."

Jackson once asked Brasseale if he could make a living running track after high school. When the coach told him no, he decided not to give up football and baseball. As a sophomore, Jackson led McAdory to the state track-and-field championship by finishing third in the ten-event decathlon competition. Some of the events, like the pole vault (12.6 feet as a senior) and the discus throw (149 feet without spinning his body), he'd never attempted until high school, but as Atchison, who was also the track coach, remarked, "It didn't matter because he could pick up a sport and do it well quicker than anybody I ever saw."

The next two years, Bo was the state decathlon champion without running the mile, the final event, because "distance is the only thing I hate about track." He set state records in the 60- and 100-yard hurdles, the long jump, and the high jump. During his senior year, he won the state triple-jump title (48 feet, 8¼ inches) and set a state record of 9.54 in the 100-yard dash on the same day. And he did all those incredible things that day on a twisted ankle.

When Bo Jackson wasn't setting records at track meets, he was a gem on the baseball diamond. Terry Brasseale took over as McAdory's baseball coach during Bo's junior year and Jackson told him, "I don't want to pitch this year. It's boring. All I do is strike them out. If you want me to pitch, I won't play."

"To be honest," Brasseale said, "Bo had a real crummy attitude when he was a junior. He could be real arrogant to the teachers. But I think that was just a defense mechanism because of his stuttering. You knew when he was telling a lie or not telling you the complete truth, because he would stutter something terrible.

"By and large, though, Bo was quiet," Brasseale added. "He wasn't a rah-rah guy, but was definitely a leader on the field. During his junior year we were on an eight-game losing streak, even though Bo was hitting home runs. We got beat this one game pretty bad and I cussed the team out and made them run laps. Bo got upset about it. I said, 'Bo, if you don't like it, you can get your ass out of here.' He started crying and said, 'Coach, I'll do anything you ask me to do. But I can't stand these guys. They're not even trying. They don't care if we win or lose.' I was really surprised to see him that way, but I didn't know Bo that well then."

Brasseale kept Bo on the mound, where he was almost unhittable during his junior and senior years. "Bo's fast ball looked like a white pea shooting at you," one hitter said.

The coach had wanted to move Bo behind the plate, but "catching would take too much out of his legs and hurt him for track." So Brasseale played Bo more at shortstop, even though Jackson didn't exactly move like Michael Jackson on certain types of ground balls. "He wasn't smooth," recalled Brasseale, "but he was so quick you couldn't hit anything by him. One time a guy hit a little shallow line drive over the second-base bag. Bo turns and runs with his back to the plate. While the second baseman is lunging for the ball, all of a sudden you see a streak flying underneath the ball. It was Bo diving from shortstop and he caught the ball right before it hit the grass."

There was also a play when a ground ball bounced off the third baseman and Bo had to backhand the ball at the edge of the outfield grass behind third. While on his knees, he pivoted and made a throw to nail the runner that never went more than a couple of feet off the ground.

But what awed Brasseale, the major-league scouts, and

Bo's teammates even more than the arm were Jackson's power and speed. Bo batted .450 his junior year and .447 as a senior, setting a national home-run record for homers in a season with 20 in only 25 games. One home run was measured at over 500 feet, and, added Brasseale, "About nineteen of those home runs were to right center field. I don't think it was from swinging late as much as being behind the fast ball. That's how strong he was. He could be overpowered by a pitcher, yet still overpower the ball out of the park."

"What he did with a bat in high school was scary," said Kenny Gonzales, who scouted Bo for the Kansas City Royals and had once been Terry Brasseale's college coach. "I laughed watching him sometimes because as a baseball player he was so crude and clumsy. But he had the bat power and speed and just crushed the ball. I remember when Bo came to bat, his coach in the third-base box would back up about ten feet because Bo hit the ball down the line so hard. I think the thing that impressed me most was that he was a man among boys."

And in four years, Jackson stole 90 bases in—get this— 91 attempts. (Wonder if some major-league team signed the catcher who threw him out.) "What was amazing about that stolen-base statistic," Brasseale revealed, "is that Bo didn't really know how to steal bases. I never got a chance to work with him a lot because when he wasn't playing a game, he was in class or running track. When I did work with him, it was trying to teach him how to take a lead and get a jump on a pitcher. He stole a lot of bases on sheer natural ability. Sometimes he wouldn't take off until the ball was halfway toward the plate and he'd still beat the throw to second."

The one display of Bo Jackson's swiftness that Brasseale remembers more than any other occurred during a county playoff game in Bo's senior year. The opposition outfield, familiar with Bo's power, was playing very deep for this particular Jackson at-bat. Bo hit a high, shallow fly ball to left field, but the left fielder was positioned near the fence about 320 feet away. What occurred next was something Brasseale claims "no one ever believes."

"The shortstop goes out for the pop and the left fielder races in," Brasseale explained. "Then they get confused on who's gonna take it and the ball falls between them. Now anytime Bo would hit a fly ball, he'd kind of loaf. He wouldn't really hustle to first. But, this being a big game, he went hard right off the bat. I'm coaching third and looking at the ball and holding my hands up to stop Bo at second, figuring he'd go for a double. But when I look toward second, he's already coming to third; he's right at me about six feet away! I was so shocked, I just pointed home and he made it without even sliding. He got there so fast there wasn't even a throw made. And it wasn't like the fielders were bobbling the ball or anything. Bo just outran the play. The stadium was packed that night and the fans were going crazy and it wasn't even our home game. Everybody knew that you just don't see someone turn a pop-up into a home run very often."

Dick Egan, a national cross-checker for the Major League Scouting Bureau, was one of the many talent experts who saw Bo play throughout his career at McAdory. Most of these scouts rate players on a numerical scale from poor to excellent, and Egan gave Jackson three eights (on a scale from two to eight) in power, arm, and speed. "His fielding was weak and his instincts were weak," Egan told *Sport* magazine in 1985, "but fielding is the easiest thing to teach, so that wasn't going to be a problem. He just had to learn the game. But the physical tools? Christ! You could scout for years and years and never see a guy like that."

Ironically, Terry Brasseale's favorite Bo Jackson story has nothing to do with his baseball, football, or track exploits. It's a basketball story and it illustrates better than any tale of Bo just how amazing his athletic talents were. One afternoon, Bo was studying in the McAdory gym. Basketball practice had ended and he was all alone except for Brasseale.

"Now, you have to realize that Bo never really cared about basketball," Brasseale related. "But on this day, he spotted a basketball on the gym floor, walked over, picked it up, and looked around to make sure nobody was watching. Then he takes a couple of steps and dunks the ball behind his head. I mean, you just don't do that when you don't play the game much. I guess he just wanted to know if he could do it."

By the time the 1982 spring semester had ended, everybody at McAdory knew that Bo Jackson would be named the school's outstanding athlete. But when the school administration announced there would be no selection for that year, black students were angry. The McAdory administration, fearful of brawls between white and black students, called an emergency meeting. As insults were exchanged, Bo Jackson stood up and quieted the inflamed crowd. "Listen, everybody," he said. "I didn't come to this school to win a popularity contest. I came for an education. Now enough of this stuff and go back to classes." Realizing the error of their ways, McAdory officials eventually gave Bo the award.

"It was an incredible moment when Bo said that," Dick Atchison recalled years later. "It stunned everybody and showed that Bo Jackson was more than just an athlete."

Four years later, after being named the winner of the Heisman Trophy as college football's outstanding player, Bo Jackson returned to McAdory to receive more than just an award. The kid who had escaped going to reform school to end up at Auburn University was honored with "Bo Jackson Day" on April 28, the day before the National Football League draft. There was a parade, a key to the city, plaques, citations, and banners reading WELCOME HOME, BO. His football jersey, number 40, was retired, the first such honor since the school started playing the sport in 1923.

"This feeling is so good," Bo told a crowd that included his family, friends, former coaches, teachers, and the current McAdory student body. "It's something I'll always cherish. You don't know how good it is to stand here at this podium. I'd like to shed a couple of tears, but I can't do that 'cause I'm a professional now. Pros don't cry."

It was at that moment, probably more than any other since he'd left McAdory in 1982, that Bo Jackson knew he had made it out of poverty, that he had kept the promise he'd made to his mother to be the first of her kids to attend college, and that in resisting the temptation to turn professional four years before, Bo Jackson had done the right thing.

Bo
Knows
College

Bo Jackson didn't just spend his senior high-school year fending off fastballs and dodging defensive linemen. As a top baseball prospect and the number-one running back contender in Alabama, he also had to stiff-arm the major-league baseball scouts and the college football recruiters who wanted to tackle him into a contract. For Bo, turning down some big-time schools like Florida, Pittsburgh, Southern Cal, and Tennessee wasn't difficult. The only place a kid from Bessemer saw himself—a kid who grew up chanting "Roll, Tide," and who idolized Coach Bear Bryant—was at the University of Alabama.

But before Bo could decide on a college, he was forced to consider an offer as tempting as a fast ball down the middle. The New York Yankees, who had scouted Bo since his junior baseball season, had selected him in the second round of the June draft. "I've seen some great hitters in my time, like Dave Winfield and Reggie Jackson," observed Yankee scout Mike Manning, "but this kid has more power and skills than either one when they were his age." The Yankees were offering Bo a quarter-million of owner George Steinbrenner's dollars. All Bo would have to do for his family to escape poverty was to sign a contract.

Bo thought about the promise he'd made to his mother about getting a college education. He thought about spending four long years in the minor leagues working his way up the pro-baseball ladder. He thought about how in those same four years he could play football, baseball, run track, *and* get a degree. He thought about how even bigger money could be his if he became a college sports star. He thought about all this and told the Yankees they had struck out. There would be no New York headlines reading "Bo and the Bo-ss."

When Bo began thinking about colleges, he scratched from his list schools like Hawaii or Florida because "they were party schools. If I'd gone there, I'da flunked out my first term." He wanted to stay in his home state and narrowed his choices to football-power Alabama and the school long considered Alabama's "stepchild"—Auburn. Bo had his heart set on playing for the Crimson Tide, but two weeks before the signing date, Alabama recruiter and assistant coach Ken Donahue allegedly told Jackson he probably wouldn't play until late in his sophomore year or early in his junior year. "But if you go to Auburn," Donahue is supposed to have said, "you'll be on a loser for four years." Meanwhile, Auburn saw Jackson as a player who could revitalize the football program, the way the great running back Herschel Walker had done at the University of Georgia. By going to Auburn, Bo would play immediately and wouldn't be "wasting two years of my life" the way he would at Alabama. And the school's second-year coach, Pat Dye, told Bo that he would be able to play football, run track, and skip spring football practice. "Roll, Tide" was no longer part of Bo Jackson's vocabulary. His motto was now, "Go, Tigers."

Jackson joined an Auburn team that had gone 5–6 in each of the previous two seasons and was considered one of the weaker teams in the Southeastern Conference. But Pat Dye, who had been a successful head coach at East Carolina and Wyoming, was determined to turn Auburn into a conference power the equal of Alabama. Dye recruited about 20 high-school football stars for the '82 season and would build around them and the highly acclaimed Bo Jackson. "This kid," Dye said, "is going to give Auburn people hope at a time they think there is no hope."

Auburn's veteran players found out how gifted their new freshman running back was during Bo's very first practice with the varsity team. The Tigers' offense ran most plays out of the "wishbone," which gave the quarterback the option of running with the ball after a sweep or pitching out to a back. Bo was playing fullback, and on the first few handoffs, junior quarterback Randy Campbell couldn't get the ball into Jackson's stomach. Campbell thought Bo was jumping too early or was lined up too close to the quarterback. The coaches checked Bo's positioning and ran the play. Again, Campbell stuck the ball into Jackson's ribs. "I said, 'Coach, you gotta get him lined up right,' " Campbell recalled. "He said, 'No, you gotta speed up.' And the coach was right. I'd never seen a freshman that was so extremely quick like Bo."

Jackson not only made the varsity; he made his first appearance in the second game of the '82 season. There were more than 60,000 fans at Auburn's Jordan-Haire Stadium when Bo was sent in against Wake Forest. "Don't be nervous," running back Lionel James told Bo. "When we pitch you the ball, haul ass."

Jackson spun and bulled his way for 11 yards on his first carry, scored on a 1-yard touchdown run on the same drive, and in the fourth quarter he outraced the entire Wake Forest defense for a 43-yard touchdown. Auburn won, 28–10, and Jackson ran for 123 yards on only 10 carries. "Go, Bo, go!" the fans had shouted all through the game. The newspapers the next day called it "The Bo Show" and everyone started comparing Jackson to Herschel Walker, the great star at Georgia. Bo Jackson, the new national football hero, discouraged the Walker talk.

"We got a sign in the locker room that says, 'Be yourself, because nobody is better qualified,' " he told the sportswriters. "Well, I'm not Herschel Walker. I'm me, Bo Jackson."

Being Bo Jackson was more than enough for fans of the Tigers. He compiled 99 yards rushing and another 59 yards returning kicks in the following week's 21–19 victory against Southern Miss. He ran for 110 yards and 111 yards in wins against Tennessee and Kentucky, respectively, before sitting out the season's sixth game against Georgia Tech with a deep thigh bruise. The injury was supposed to keep Jackson sidelined for the next game against Mississippi State, but with Auburn trailing, 17–14, in the third quarter, coach Pat Dye gambled that Bo could turn the game around. He was right. Bo's presence ignited the team. He ran for 59 yards in 8 carries and led Auburn to 21 fourth-quarter points and a victory.

The next week, Auburn lost to Florida, 19–17, and Pat Dye tongue-lashed his team for its listless play. He was especially critical of Jackson, who had gained only 23 yards, and Bo responded the following week with a 114-yard effort against Rutgers. Everyone had hoped Jackson would duplicate that performance in the upcoming confrontation with Georgia and Herschel Walker. The game would also be vital to Auburn's chances for a major bowl berth. But Bo wasn't up to the challenge in a game dubbed "The Walker-Jackson Duel." While Walker toyed with

Auburn's defense, gaining 177 yards and scoring 2 touchdowns, Jackson rushed for only 58 yards in 14 carries and Auburn lost, 19–14.

Bo was distraught after the Georgia game. Not only had he been stifled as a ball carrier, but he made what one coach called "a ton of mistakes." Pat Dye and his assistants worked Bo hard in practice the next couple of days, so hard that Jackson couldn't take it anymore. He hated practice, and the fans and the press were on his back. He was lonely, he was homesick, and he decided to quit. Bo packed his bags, borrowed a friend's car, and drove to the Greyhound bus station, where he sat on a bench for hours just thinking. He thought about going back home for good, but realized he wouldn't get anywhere without his college degree. "I don't want to end up like the other guys from the neighborhood," he reasoned. Finally, at a little past midnight, a station agent chased him out and he called an assistant coach who talked him into going back to campus. The next day, Pat Dye told Bo that the staff would ease off on him in practice, but that for breaking curfew he'd have to run hundreds of "stadiums," which were sprints up and down the stadium steps. Dye also told Bo that he was the one player who gave Auburn a chance to beat Alabama and become the best team in the state.

The rivalry between Alabama and Auburn may well be the most intense in college football because unlike Army-Navy, Michigan–Ohio State, Notre Dame–Southern California, it is a state intramural battle, the sports Civil War of Dixie. The entire area comes to a stop when Alabama and Auburn go at each other. The Tide-Tigers confrontation began in 1893 and it was sometime during the 1950s that long-time Auburn coach Shug Jordan began calling it the "Iron Bowl." Writer Geoffrey Norman, who authored a book about the rivalry, called *Alabama Showdown*, wrote

31

that the name "Iron Bowl" was "an accurate reflection of the spirit of the game as well as the tough, dirty, hard-nosed steel town in which it is played."

Bo Jackson had never worked so hard or been so motivated for a game in his young career. As he practiced, he thought about the Alabama recruiter who'd told him Auburn wouldn't beat Alabama in Bo's four years at the school. Jackson was intent upon making that coach eat his words and ending Auburn's nine-year losing streak against the Tide. "Just watch Bo against Alabama," Pat Dye was saying as he observed Bo practice. "It's like something happened to him overnight."

With more than 76,000 screaming fans in Birmingham's Legion Field, the teams exchanged first-quarter touchdowns. In the second quarter, Auburn went up, 14–13, but Alabama regained the lead in the third, 22–14, on a touchdown and a field goal. A failed two-point conversion on the touchdown, however, would come back to haunt the Tide.

Over the first three quarters, Alabama's tough defense had held Jackson to just about 50 yards rushing, Bo's longest jaunt gaining only 12. But at the start of the last quarter, and with Auburn holding the ball on its own 33, Bo began to put on a running clinic. On the second play of the drive, Randy Campbell pitched the ball out to Bo, who was sprinting toward the left sideline. Bo then suddenly bolted upfield, found a hole, and evaded tacklers coming from all angles. Bo wasn't stopped until he'd gained 53 yards and had brought the ball to Alabama's 13-yard line. A few plays later a field goal made the score 22–17, but the Tigers still needed a touchdown to win.

Auburn forced the Tide to punt on its next possession and took over the ball on Alabama's 34 with just over 7 minutes in the game. First Jackson kept the drive alive with a 3-yard run on a fourth and one from the 'Bama 45. Then a 16-yard pass completion and a pass interference penalty gave Auburn the ball on Alabama's 9-yard line. After a Tigers penalty brought the ball back to the 14, Bo's 5-yard run and an 8-yard pass from Campbell to Jackson (only a great tackle stopped Bo from scoring) put the ball inches from the goal line.

It was the fourth down with only 2 minutes and 30 seconds left in the game. In the huddle, Campbell called "Play 43," which meant "Bo over the top." Nobody had been able to stop the play all season. Jackson took the handoff up over the line and jumped just enough to score what proved to be the winning touchdown in Auburn's 23–22 victory. The Tide's hex over the Tigers was history, as were the Legion Field goalposts and Alabama's legendary coach, Bear Bryant, who retired days after the game. Auburn was now the football power of Alabama.

"We had made up our minds that we were going to score," Bo said after the game. He had gained 114 yards on 17 carries and was named the game's Most Valuable Player. "Nobody was going to stop us. Nobody was going to stop me. I knew I was going to have to jump as high as I ever jumped to get over. We were going to win this game."

Bo finished his freshman football season with 829 yards and 9 touchdowns and then ran for 64 more yards in a 33–26 victory over Boston College in the Tangerine Bowl (which gave Auburn a 9–3 season). Quarterback Randy Campbell remembered one play from that Bowl game, which for him captured the essence of Jackson's talent. "We had a third and goal to go from the nine," Campbell recalled, "and we couldn't stick it in. Coach Dye said, 'I don't care what happens, pitch the ball to Bo.' I rolled left and saw the defensive end run toward Bo, who was flared outside. So I pitched the ball back more than I wanted to so it wouldn't be deflected. While moving forward, Bo reached back and one-handed it with his right hand. Then he broke three tackles while straddling the sideline and ran in for a touchdown. You just can't do something like that.''

After his first successful football season, Bo played baseball and ran track, making him the SEC's first three-sport letterman in 20 years. In both 1983 and 1984, Jackson qualified for the NCAA indoor final in the 60-yard dash. In 1984, he was a member of the Tiger's 4 times 100 outdoor relay team and ran a 10.39 in the 100 meters at the Florida Relays. He sat out the 1984 baseball season, hoping to run for the 1984 United States Olympic track team, but just missed qualifying, primarily because he'd been so preoccupied with football and classes.

As for baseball, track had cut into Bo's 1983 season, and when he did finally join the team, he struck out in his first 21 times at bat. But again, showing the extraordinary natural ability that would become his trademark, Bo recovered to hit .279 with 4 home runs playing in just 26 of Auburn's 50 games. In one contest in Tuscaloosa, he responded to the crew of a beer truck taunting ''boy'' at him beyond the outfield fence by smashing a home run against the truck. Two springs later, Bo joined the baseball team again ''to have something to occupy my time.'' And without track to distract him, Bo exhibited the awesome potential that had major-league scouts drooling. In 42 games as the Tigers' starting center fielder, Bo batted .401 with 17 homers in 147 at-bats, 5 doubles, 6 triples, a team-leading 55 runs scored, and 43 RBI's.

Bo's legendary game that season occurred on April 2 at Georgia's Foley Field. In the fourth inning, Jackson hit a ball into an 85-foot-high bank of lights over the 375-foot sign in left center field. People who saw the blast swear the ball was still rising when it hit the lights. "They had just christened that new lighting system before the game," Auburn baseball coach Hal Baird remembered. "It knocked out one of the lights. It was like in the movie *The Natural.* There were a couple of seconds of silence—people just watching—and then a standing ovation. After that Bo hit two more homers and two doubles. His flair for the dramatic was never more evident than on that night."

Baird, who had been a pitcher in the Kansas City Royals organization in the seventies, joined the growing list of people awed by Bo's unrefined baseball talent.

"In seven years in pro baseball," he told *Sports Illustrated,* "I saw four or five guys, total, who had the type of power Bo possesses; three or four who could run like he can; and three or four who could throw like he can. But those were twelve different people. It sounds like I'm talking about Superman."

But it was on a football field where Bo Jackson could appear faster than a speeding bullet, more powerful than a locomotive, and be able to leap tall middle linebackers in a single bound. He started the '83 season about where he left off in '82. In an opening-game victory against Southern Miss, he ran for 73 yards on only 11 carries. But in the next week's 20–7 loss to Texas, he got the ball only seven times and gained just 35 yards. Coach Dye admitted afterward that getting Bo the ball so few times was "a mistake that won't happen again." Jackson averaged 13 carries a game for the rest of the year and Auburn didn't lose another game, finishing with an 11–1 record and an SEC championship.

Bo ran for a conference-high 1,213 yards, a 7.7 yards-per-carry average, and 12 touchdowns. He produced five 100-plus yard games, including a 196-yard effort against Florida (scoring on 55- and 80-yard touchdown runs) while suffering from a virus. Then in the '83 Iron Bowl against Alabama, Bo romped for a 69-yard touchdown after reversing his field on an abortive sweep, and later dashed for a 71-yard TD, leading Auburn to a 23–20 come-from-behind victory. All told, Bo ran for 256 yards on 20 carries in the game that put the Tigers into the Sugar Bowl against Big Ten champion Michigan and gave the team a shot at the national championship.

In the weeks before the Sugar Bowl, Bo basked in the glory of being everybody's All-American. In Hollywood he was honored as a member of the Kodak Coaches and Associated Press All-American teams. And everywhere Bo went, people wanted to know how the football player who turned the fastest 40-yard-dash time ever on a football field (4.1), and had led the SEC in four categories, had evolved as a runner.

"When I came to Auburn," Bo revealed, "I was a vertical runner. Now I run tilted at my shoulders, with authority. My freshman year I was running scared. But after I got hit in the 'Bama game and fumbled, I said '*No* more. I'm not gonna take no more licks.' You can't be a good back if guys dog you out every time you got the ball."

Auburn offensive coordinator Jack Crowe explained that because Bo was an unpolished runner out of high school, he had to learn a running style as he went along. "He started this season trying to knock folks down," Crowe said. "By the second half, he was giving defenses the fast track instead of the hard road."

When Bo returned to Auburn, he not only had to prepare for action with Michigan, but had to answer questions about the latest controversy. Robert Irsay, the owner of the NFL's Baltimore Colts, had leaked a story claiming that he was negotiating a deal with Jackson to join his team. Irsay, who had a reputation for being something of a loose cannon, was engaged in a contract battle with his star running back, Curtis Dickey. He said he wouldn't pay Dickey $4 million if he could get Jackson for $2.5 million. Bo vehemently denied the rumor.

"I've never met the man," he insisted. "I never talked to anyone about turning pro. I don't want to jeopardize my eligibility. I'm very happy being at Auburn. I plan to get my degree. That's what my mother wants, too." Bo's teammates and Coach Dye believed and supported him.

"Bo will be in the running for the Heisman Trophy his next two years," the coach said. "For this to come up, it's just stupid."

And quarterback Randy Campbell added: "We don't believe it because we know Bo. But if it had been true, it sure would have changed our game plan for the Sugar Bowl."

The game against Michigan was a bruising affair that was dominated by the defense and the running backs. Bo led Auburn to a 9–7 victory and a ranking of third in the nation with a 130-yard effort on 22 carries. He was cited as the game's Most Valuable Player, but in the locker room he handed the trophy to his roommate, senior back Lionel James, whose tough runs had kept Auburn in the game. Bo could afford to be gracious about this particular award. He knew that in the next two years he could capture an even more prestigious piece of hardware—the Heisman Trophy.

Bo
Knows
the Heisman

The Bo Jackson-for-the-1984-Heisman hype began in earnest when *Sports Illustrated* profiled college football's latest star in its annual football preview issue. The opening photo portrait next to the headline "Bo on the Go" was that of a tough, yet nonmenacing young black man in a tanktop T-shirt. Beads of sweat dripped from Bo's unblemished face to his massive neck and a straw dangled provocatively from the side of his mouth. Bo knows poses. The magazine proclaimed that Bo Jackson was "the straw that stirs the drink" at Auburn, a statement tinged with irony since the man responsible for that famous quote, baseball legend Reggie Jackson, was one of Bo's idols.

The article gave readers the obligatory glimpse of Jackson's interests and habits. When Bo wasn't chewing up yardage, he gnawed on straws to help him relax, especially during a school exam. Bo tried to evade women who would "stop at nothing to get you for your name or popularity." Bo's musical taste leaned more toward gospel than rock and roll, and he liked playing video games. And, of course, Bo loved kids and would preach to them about staying out of trouble. Mostly, however, the article rehashed Jackson's exploits in athletics, the stories that had made him, in the magazine's words, "a legend in Alabama and this season's hottest Heisman candidate."

Many people thought Bo had a chance to become the first player since Ohio State's Archie Griffin in 1974 and 1975 to win *two* Heismans. To help him in that quest, and to give Auburn a better shot at the national title, Pat Dye planned to have Bo carry the ball more in 1984. In the wishbone offense, as opposed to the "I" that Herschel Walker ran in at Georgia, Bo got fewer chances, but could break more long runs. Dye wanted to increase Bo's average carries per game from 15 to 25. If Jackson could maintain his 6.5- to 7.5-yards-per-carry average, he could get about 175 yards a game.

Auburn opened its season against the previous year's national champion, Miami, in the Kickoff Classic. For Bo Jackson and the Tigers, it was not a ferocious start. Miami won the game, 20–18, and although Bo ran for 96 yards on 20 carries, he twisted his ankle midway through the game. Bo limped around while practicing for the next game against Texas, and teammates urged him to sit one out. "People get injured when they try to play in pain," he was told. But Bo was determined to avenge the last season's Texas loss even it meant risking a more serious injury.

Bo was running well early in the game and had scored a first-quarter touchdown. Then it happened. At the end of a classic 53-yard Jackson romp, which saw him cut up the middle and then down the right sideline, Auburn's number-one ranking and Bo's Heisman hopes died under a pile of bodies in Austin.

At some point during Bo's sideline jaunt, pain shot through his bad ankle, causing him to slow down just enough for Texas safety Jerry Gray to grab him from behind at the knees. Bo went down hard, his right shoulder slamming against the Texas turf. Wincing from the pain, Bo got up slowly and ran a few more plays before sitting out the rest of the game. With Bo out for the second half, Auburn lost, 35–27. Now the only question was: Would the season be lost? When the X rays on Bo's shoulder came in, they revealed a separation, an injury that would most likely sideline him for the rest of the season. There would be no Heisman for Bo Jackson in 1984. And that night the former bully from Bessemer cried like a baby.

No longer a candidate for the Heisman, Bo threw his support to Boston College quarterback Doug Flutie. Jackson phoned Flutie and jokingly told him not to catch the Heisman "virus" that had infected him and Navy running back Napoleon McCallum, who'd also been sidelined by injury. "I want Doug to win the Heisman because he's a class person and a great competitor," said Bo, who caught Flutie's flamboyant act in the 1982 Tangerine Bowl. "I think he's the most exciting player in the game." (Flutie would end up winning the 1984 Heisman.)

While waiting for his shoulder to heal, Bo devoted more time to his classes and to romantic pursuits. Studying one day in the Auburn student lounge, he met an attractive young woman named Linda Garrett, who was working on her doctorate in counseling psychology. They attended the same child-development classes, and after a while Bo began taking his textbooks to Linda's apartment to study. Linda Garrett realized that Bo Jackson wasn't just another one-track-mind athlete—a.k.a. dumb jock.

"Bo was such a nice guy," Linda told the *Birmingham Post-Herald* in 1989. "We were friends for a couple of months before the love thing started. We'd go to lunch and he'd tell me about his dates. Then things started to feel different between us."

40

Things also started to feel different between Bo's neck and shoulder and he shocked Auburn's trainers by suiting up after only six weeks on the sidelines. The Tigers had won all six games in Bo's absence, and although the Heisman was no longer attainable, a major Bowl berth was still within reach. Besides, how could Bo possibly miss a confrontation with Alabama? Three games would give Bo more than enough preparation for the Iron Bowl.

Pat Dye worked Jackson slowly back into the offense. Bo carried the ball only five times for 16 yards in a 24–3 loss to Florida, eight times for 57 yards and 3 touchdowns in a 60–0 slaughter of Cincinnati, and 18 times for 87 yards in a 21–12 victory over Georgia. With Bo getting back into top form, 8–3 Auburn felt confident that it would beat 4–6 Alabama to win another SEC championship and make another Sugar Bowl appearance.

But those accomplishments were not meant to be in 1984. As the Iron Bowl would make plain, it was certainly not Bo Jackson's year. Alabama was leading, 17–15, in the fourth quarter, but Bo was having a good day. He had run for over 100 yards (one was a 28-yard scamper) and scored a touchdown. Then midway through the quarter, Auburn intercepted a pass and returned the ball to the 'Bama 17. Three minutes later, the Tigers were faced with a fourth down from Alabama's one-yard line. Everyone in Legion Field expected that Pat Dye would send in the field-goal unit, since a three-pointer would put Auburn up by one. But Dye decided to, as one Auburn insider said, "run the ball down Alabama's throat, which would have given him more satisfaction than all the field goals in the world."

When the kicking team didn't run on the field, the entire stadium and a national television audience thought they would see Bo run over the top. Instead, Dye sent in a play that called for back Brent Fullwood to sweep right in front of Jackson's block. But Bo never heard the signals, and when the ball was snapped he went left while Fullwood went right. Without the fullback out front to cut down the safety, Fullwood was ridden out of bounds for a loss. The controversial call became known as "The Play," and Coach Dye and Jackson became the state's biggest jokes. "How do you get to Auburn from Memphis? Go to the one-yard line and turn left."

Instead of playing in New Orleans on New Year's Day, Auburn faced Arkansas in the more lowly Liberty Bowl. Bo managed to salvage some pride by gaining 88 yards and taking the game's MVP in a 21–15 victory, but he still couldn't help thinking that, for him, 1984 had been a major disappointment. It would be a long off-season. Even when he was on the baseball field that spring, Bo couldn't help thinking about getting another chance at capturing the Heisman.

But two teams wanted to put different thoughts in Bo's head; thoughts that involved money instead of trophies. After the '84 football season, the Birmingham Stallions of the two-year-old United States Football League offered Jackson half a million dollars to quit Auburn and play pro ball in Alabama. The USFL had already signed Herschel Walker and running back Marcus Dupree after their junior years, and now they wanted to make Jackson jump. Bo admitted the offer was tempting, but he turned Birmingham down. After all, he figured, a big-bucks offer from an NFL team would certainly come his way after next year's draft.

Then in June 1985, after his impressive baseball season, the California Angels selected Bo in the twentieth round of the baseball draft and told him he could be playing in the majors by 1986. The Angels were hoping that Jackson would be willing to challenge an SEC rule that prohibited athletes from playing one sport as a professional, while retaining amateur status in another sport. Pacific Ten quarterback John Elway of Stanford had once played college football the same year in which he was a minor-league player for the New York Yankees. Bo realized that in the SEC, signing a contract would disqualify him for playing football. He told the Angels he wouldn't even talk money with them. He was intent on setting Auburn rushing records and winning the Heisman.

Pay Dye was willing to do anything necessary to help Bo achieve his goals. First, he changed the Auburn offense from the wishbone to the "I" formation. In the "I," Bo would be the featured back on almost all running plays, and Dye hoped that would translate into more yards. Then Dye did something that went against his firm belief in hard work and angered some members of the team. Dye knew Bo hated the regimentation of football practice and that he had sculpted a rock-solid body without lifting weights or doing formal exercises. So he let Bo skip weight-training sessions and allowed him to practice at his own pace.

"I have never in my life been around an athlete like that," Dye told *Sport* magazine. "I wish you'd tell me how to train a guy like that to run the football and be the best he can be on Saturday because I don't know. I think he has tuned that body and he knows how that body responds better than I do. I think you're fooling with some very delicate mental and physical preparations when a guy like that gets ready to play. And I'm not going to question him as long as he's not a distraction to the other coaches and players."

Dye's strategy for Bo was an immediate success. Jackson ran like a wild boar in the 49–7 opening-game victory against Southwest Louisiana. He gained 290 yards on 23 carries, with touchdown runs of 7, 47, 76, and 12 yards.

Bo followed that with a superb 205-yard, 2-touchdown effort in a 29–18 win over Southern Mississippi. He had broken out to a huge lead in the Heisman race, and the next game would be broadcast on national television against underdog Tennessee. But after gaining almost 80 yards on 16 carries by early in the third quarter, Bo pulled up lame after having been cut down at the knees on his seventeenth run. He limped out of the game, never to return. Bo had remembered what happened the last time he played hurt, and he wasn't about to risk the rest of the season or his future. After Auburn lost, 38–20, dropping them from the number-one spot in the national rankings, Bo was blasted by the media for not playing with pain. The media raised questions about Bo's character that would dog him all the way to Heisman voting day.

Bo rebounded with four successive Heisman-caliber performances. In Auburn victories over Mississippi, Florida State, Georgia Tech, and Mississippi State, Jackson ran for 240, 176, 242, and 169 yards, respectively. He scored a total of 7 touchdowns in the 4 games, one as long as 76 yards. But while practicing for the game against Florida, a national-championship contender, Bo badly bruised his thigh again. Though his leg wasn't in optimum condition by game time, he bravely tried playing against Florida. After struggling for just 48 yards on 15 carries in the first half, his lowest total of the season, he took himself out of the game with a minute left. His thigh just couldn't take the pounding anymore.

"I caught somebody's knee between my thigh pad and my knee pad," he told the trainer working on his leg in the locker room. Bo tried to play again with five minutes left in the game, but the thigh spasmed up. He came out of the game for good and Auburn ended up losing in the fourth quarter, 14–10. The Tigers had been defeated in both games in which Bo rushed for under 100 yards, and now their national championship chances were dead.

The Alabama writers tried to kill Bo's Heisman hopes, too, and they jumped on Jackson the way players pile up at the goal line. Again, his critics said Bo was a quitter. They wondered how they could vote for a Heisman candidate who couldn't play with the small hurts. Bo Jackson jokes started circulating throughout the state. "You heard about the new kind of Auburn ice cream?" began one. "It's called the Bosicle. Two licks and it's gone."

Sports columnists debated about Bo's character in the Alabama papers as if it were an issue of national importance. "People take some things in life for granted," wrote Paul Finebaum of the *Birmingham Post-Herald*. "Death and taxes. Hot summers, cold winters. Now, there's a new one—Bo Jackson pulling a disappearing act in critical football games. . . . Jackson remains the leading candidate for the Heisman Trophy, but it's unlikely he's a serious threat for a Purple Heart. . . . Perhaps he ought to give up football and concentrate on baseball, which is not so taxing on the body."

Kevin Scarbinsky of the *Birmingham News* rebutted by writing: "Only a bone sticking through Bo's flesh would satisfy critics that he can play hurt. . . . Jackson toughs it out and plays every Saturday even though every squad wants a shot at the Heisman candidate like hunters going after big game. . . . To say Bo chokes in big games is a cruel joke. . . . Bo Jackson not only deserves the Heisman, he deserves the chance to fail and not have people hate him for it."

Pat Dye jumped to Jackson's defense by reminding the critics about how Bo came back early from a separated shoulder the previous year for the Florida game. "Everybody expects him to be Superman," Dye said. "They

45

don't realize he's got blood vessels and bones and muscles that can bruise and break like everybody else does."

For his part, Bo tried to remain cool despite all the criticism. This was no time to incur the wrath of the Heisman electorate. "I do sustain bruises and stuff," he said. "I will break. And I just know when I can play and when I can't play. But you'll always have those people out there who will criticize Auburn or criticize Bo Jackson if we lose. I look at all the people doing the criticizing—they never played a down of football. All I know is that I am not a quitter. I'm not a coward. But maybe now I have to go out and prove myself all over again."

Auburn's trainers worked on Bo's thigh all week prior to the next game, against East Carolina, but could only get his leg up to about 60 percent flexibility. Still, Bo toughed out 73 yards on 14 carries in the first half of an eventual 35–10 victory. Pat Dye then kept Bo out most of the second half. He wanted to be sure Bo was as healthy as possible for the big national television game against Georgia, and for the Iron Bowl game a week later. It would be Bo's last two chances to prove he was worthy of the Heisman.

Bo rested his leg during the week of the Georgia game and then came up with a clutch performance against the best defense in the Conference. He ran for 121 yards on 19 carries and scored 2 touchdowns, 1 TD coming on a 67-yard scamper in which he zigzagged, made cutbacks, and broke tackles all the way down the field. The other touchdown came from inside the ten and was even more impressive. With two defenders between him and the goal, Bo ran over one without losing his balance or momentum, then shook out of the grasp of the second tackler and bounced into the end zone. The combined effect of Bo's touchdown runs displayed everything one could ask for in a Heisman Trophy running back—speed, quickness, agility, deceptiveness, strength, power, and determination. On top of all that, Bo made his incredible second touchdown run while seriously injured. Three days after the Georgia game, the Auburn team physician told Bo he had played the second half with two broken ribs. Who said this guy couldn't play with pain?

It certainly wasn't Pat Dye, who, in the days prior to the 1985 Iron Bowl, verbally cast his very partial vote for the Heisman. "Tell me something," Dye said to some Tigers boosters at a Birmingham Touchdown Club meeting, "do you believe there is any way, after Georgia, that the Yankee press can give the Heisman to anybody but Bo?" When somebody mentioned Iowa quarterback Chuck Long, Dye responded with, "Shee-it! Did you see that sumbitch Bo run? And he was running against Georgia, the junkyard dogs themselves. He wasn't running against the Sweetbriar Sissies. I've watched a lot of 'em, back to Billy Cannon, and I believe Bo is the best. I never saw Herschel get any tougher yards than them that Bo got on Saturday. Last week, before Georgia, I was reading all about how Bo ain't got no guts. Well, last week Bo Jackson left his guts all over the field. And he's going to help himself even more this Saturday against Aladamnbama. Think about the worst day Bo's ever had against the Tide. One hundred and fourteen yards. They'll be lucky if he don't double it."

Well, Bo didn't double his yardage total, but he had a Heisman-caliber day in what many Alabamians felt was the most exciting Iron Bowl ever played.

With a packed house at Legion Field and a national television audience watching, Bo found the yardage hard to come by as an inspired Alabama squad jumped out to a surprising 10–0 lead in the first quarter. "They don't believe they can win!" shouted an Alabama player on the sideline. And an ABC reporter said the Auburn players were "in shock."

But after Alabama had to settle for another field goal, a Tide booster said, "You can't be satisfied with field goals when you play Auburn. You know that their big guy is going to break one sooner or later."

Sure enough, on the Tigers' next possession, Bo went into another gear. He capped an Auburn touchdown drive with a seven-yard run during which he barreled over two Alabama defenders before reaching the end zone. Then, with the Tide leading, 16–10, in the fourth quarter, Bo sparked an Auburn drive with one tough run after another. He broke tackles and ran over people and was seeming to get stronger as the game progressed. Bo showed the fans and media that he was one of the most dangerous runners in football when, on third and 19 from the Alabama 25, he took a dropoff pass and carried it down to the 6. Three plays later, Auburn was faced with a fourth down from the half-yard line. That year, it was not Bo blocking for somebody else, it was Bo over the top. The extra point made it 17–16, Auburn, with less than seven minutes left.

Alabama had plenty of time to score, but they didn't have a Bo Jackson. Then, amazingly, a freshman halfback named Gene Jelks showed he knew Bo impressions. Jelks took a routine pitchout and outran the overshifted Auburn defense for a 74-yard touchdown that sent Legion Field into a frenzy. After failing on a two-point conversion attempt, the Tide led, 22–17.

When Auburn got the ball back with about five minutes left, they turned to—who else?—the bodacious one. In between a couple of pass plays, Bo ran for four, two, five, and six yards before carrying the ball to the one-yard line with a minute left. Then running back Reggie Ware took the ball in for the go-ahead touchdown. After the two-pointer failed, Auburn was leading, 23–22. Bo stood on the sidelines, leading the Auburn fans' deafening cheers by waving a towel in circles over his head.

But Alabama wasn't about to throw in their towels just yet. Facing a third and 18 from its own 12-yard line with just 37 seconds left, the Tide converted 2 plays worth 34 yards. Then quarterback Mike Shula completed a pass, giving Alabama the ball on the Auburn 35 with 6 seconds remaining and the clock moving. The Tide field-goal team raced onto the field and, with the entire stadium on its feet, kicker Van Tifflin booted a perfect 52-yard field goal. Alabama won, 25–23, with no time left on the clock.

The morning after, Alabama coach Ray Perkins not only reveled in his team's unlikely comeback victory, but he talked admiringly about Bo Jackson. Perkins was impressed with how Bo ran for 142 yards and 2 touchdowns in 31 carries, even though he was still suffering from broken ribs. "You know," Perkins said, "I'd like to be that man's agent. Bo Jackson is the best running back in the world, college or pro."

As the December 7 Heisman announcement neared, few could deny that Bo had impeccable credentials for the award. His 1,786 yards gained for the 1985 season (the best single-season total in Auburn history and second-best in SEC history) gave him 4,303 lifetime yards, making him Auburn's all-time leading rusher. Only two other SEC players—Herschel Walker and Louisiana State's Charles Alexander—had ever rushed for more than 4,000 yards in a career. His 8 100-yard-plus games in '85 and 21 lifetime were both Auburn records, and his career yards-per-game average was an astounding 113.2. And, naturally, Bo was named a first-team All-American by every major poll and news organization.

But *Sports Illustrated* wasn't much impressed by all of Bo's records and accolades. In a cover story called "The Thinking Fan's Vote for the 1985 Heisman Trophy," the magazine claimed that Plymouth State running back Joe Dudek, a Division III player, for goodness' sake, was a more worthy Heisman candidate than Bo Jackson. The magazine once again raised the issue of Jackson's toughness and dedication and dismissed his injuries as "bruises."

"In two games of mortal consequence to Auburn fans this season," the magazine article stated, "Bo yanked himself out. Whatever happened to being carried off the field, you say? In big games, Bo grabs more bench time than [Supreme Court Justice] Sandra Day O'Connor. . . . Jackson took Auburn out of the Sugar Bowl with two Bo boo-boos."

"That *Sports Illustrated* story was a cheap shot," writer Geoffrey Norman quoted an Auburn booster saying in *Alabama Showdown*. "Let me tell you something about Bo Jackson's guts. Last year, when he dislocated his shoulder against Texas, he ran three more plays before he even said anything to anybody. That man has all the guts in the world. Between the sidelines, he's as tough as they come."

On the evening before the Heisman announcement, Bo went to bed early but tossed and turned more than he ever had on a football field. He woke up at five A.M. and talked with friends on the phone for two hours. Then he called his mom and told her he was scared. "Don't worry, Bo," she told her son. "Just pray and take everything as it comes."

At four-thirty that afternoon, 250 people crowded into

the Heisman Room of New York's Downtown Athletic Club. Bo looked around the room at the portraits of the previous Heisman winners. He noticed a picture of Pat Sullivan, the Auburn quarterback who won the 1971 Heisman, hanging on a pillar above a table where the 1985 trophy sat. Later he would say that "I never got nervous, even before a big game. But today I thought my heart was going to jump out of my shirt."

Auburn's associate athletic director, Oval Jaynes, said, "This is like a trial, waiting for the jury to come in."

Back in Bessemer, fifty of Bo's friends and relatives, reporters and photographers, filled the living room of his mother's old house, their eyes glued to the television. Florence Bond had a "Bo Jackson for the Heisman" button pinned to her blouse, and Bo's father, A. D. Adams, stared silently at the TV. At Auburn, hundreds of students and Bo's Tiger teammates packed the athletic dorm, ready for a wild celebration.

At five-fifty-five P.M. New York time, a Downtown Athletic Club official stepped to the podium and revealed that the election had been the closest in Heisman history. "And the winner of the 1985 Heisman Trophy is—Bo Jackson of Auburn." Bo had beaten Iowa quarterback Chuck Long by just 64 votes.

"All right! He did it!" screamed one of Bo's sisters back in Bessemer.

"I feel like I just received the Heisman myself!" said Auburn quarterback Pat Washington back at the athletic dorm.

"Now I'll be able to tell my grandchildren I played in the same backfield with a Heisman Trophy winner!" said Auburn running back Kyle Collins.

"Ever since he was little," said Bo's mom, "I had a sense that God had something special in store for him."

As everyone in the Downtown AC cheered, cameras snapped frantically and reporters went after Bo as if they were ready to gang-tackle him. They found out Bo's favorite food was liver, that he hated spinach, that his favorite sports were fishing and hunting, that he liked watching "That's Incredible" and "The Cosby Show." They also found out Bo Jackson was a very proud individual.

"The bitter memories of this season made winning the Heisman that much sweeter," he told the reporters. "I wish I could see all those people's faces, the ones who do all the criticizing, not of me, but of the coaches and the players. I wouldn't say it's a payback. I'd say it's more like getting even.

"I started at the bottom," he added. "Literally at the bottom. And I had to fight my way to the top."

Bo was introduced to the former New York Yankees broadcaster and famous Alabamian Mel Allen, who expressed the hope that Bo would play major-league baseball. "And if you do, I hope it's for the Yankees," Allen said.

Then the reporters began badgering Bo with what would become one of the most intriguing and most asked sports question of the decade. In which sport would he become a professional: football or baseball? With the NFL draft coming up in April and the baseball draft in June, Bo would have a decision to make. What would his sport of choice be? Would it depend on the money?

What Bo decided to do was to have some fun with the reporters. As he had done before many times when the issue came up, he grabbed a cowboy hat and jokingly told the media that when the time came, he would put the names of the two sports in a hat and draw one. Then, getting serious, he said plainly, "I am not going to decide what I'm going to do until after next spring's baseball season.''

All that answer did was give hundreds of sportswriters in America almost six months to try to make the decision for him.

Bo
Knows
the Pros

On New Year's Eve 1985, wouldn't it have been nice to be in Bo Jackson's Nikes? Instead of making mundane resolutions about quitting smoking or losing weight, you would have had to resolve whether to make millions playing football or make millions playing baseball. That was the decision Bo Jackson would wrestle with from the moment the Heisman hullabaloo began until the baseball draft in early June. And in between, there would be a lot of people trying to pin him to the career mat.

Bo didn't have much time to think about resolutions. His New Year's Day would be spent playing in the Cotton Bowl clash against Southwest Conference champion Texas A&M. Auburn lost the game, 36–16, and although they were knocked out of the national top-20 rankings, Bo was named the game's Most Valuable Player (his third straight Bowl game honor) for gaining 129 yards and scoring 2 touchdowns.

Once the football helmet was put away, Bo's baseball cap came out. Jackson's goals for the '86 Auburn baseball season were to surpass his stellar '85 statistics and to impress major-league clubs that he was indeed first-round draft material. But while Bo prepared for the summer game, everyone else played a guessing game—the one called "Which way will Bo go?" Surprisingly, Jackson didn't yet have an agent, but one would never know that by reading all the stories dealing with The Big Question. It seemed that everybody in sports wanted to give Bo advice about which career road he should travel. And they weren't even in line for a percentage.

"Selfishly, I think he should play football," said Gil Brandt, then player personnel director for the NFL's Dallas Cowboys. "I know that he'll be an impact player and a superstar in the NFL."

"I'd advise Bo to take a hard look at the benefits of a baseball career," pitched in Boston Red Sox general manager Lou Gorman. "Baseball salaries in the last ten years have risen five hundred percent. The pension plan is spectacular. You're not always subject to pounding and injury, and the average career is much longer in baseball than in football. It's a great life."

The Pittsburgh Pirates owned the first pick of the '86 draft, and although it would have been quite a leap to think of the inexperienced Jackson as the nation's best player, the Pirates weren't discounting the idea. "We're certainly going to take a hard look at Bo," admitted Pirates general manager Syd Thrift. "The big question is: What's in his heart? I think we'd have to have reasonable assurance that he was committed to play baseball. He needs to decide whether he wants a baseball challenge for life, or whether he'll play the other game."

California Angels scouting director Larry Himes, who was responsible for drafting Jackson the year before, believed Bo would choose fall ball over the summer game. "I think it's almost cut-and-dried he's going to the NFL," Himes said early in 1986. "I don't think he's going to be able to resist the hoopla and the dollars that go with the NFL draft and becoming an immediate starter. I don't think the baseball team that drafts him is going to be able to compete moneywise, and he'd probably have to spend some years in the minors.''

Everyone seemed to agree that as a certain number-one NFL pick, Bo could get more money from football than baseball. But nobody ruled out the possibility of a bidding war for Bo's services. If that was Bo's plan, he wasn't letting on, at least until after the college baseball season. He was dodging the issue better than an open-field runner. ''I don't think he's being secretive,'' said Auburn coach Hal Baird. ''I think he just doesn't know what he's gonna do.''

The poor media. All they could get out of Bo were quotes like, ''To me it's all about making a living. It's like choosing one job from another—working in a steel mill or a sawmill. It's just whichever one you want to get into.''

Bo had always been prone to slow starts playing baseball, and all the speculation swirling around him made concentration even more difficult. In his first 21 games, Bo batted just .246 on 17-for-69, with 7 home runs, 14 RBI's, and 30 strikeouts. For a college senior, those were not first-round-pick stats. Now, even if he denounced football, it was doubtful Bo would go early in the baseball draft. Los Angeles Dodgers manager Tommy Lasorda said he had seen Class-A minor-leaguers who were better than Jackson. Bo's baseball stock dropped even more when, after that twenty-first game, he was declared ineligible for the rest of the season. Bo said he didn't know he had broken an SEC rule by accepting transportation from the NFL's Tampa Bay Buccaneers so he could take a physical before the league's draft. (The Bucs owned the first pick and were planning to make Bo their choice.) Months later

Sports Illustrated reported that the Bucs claimed they checked with the conference before sending a private plane—which Jackson allegedly requested—to fly Bo to Tampa. In any event, the SEC ruling knocked the wind out of Bo more than any tackle could have. He cried for the first time since his junior-year football injury.

"It was a tragedy," Hal Baird said. "At first, he was really torn up about it, and that told me how much he had wanted to play baseball this spring. This makes a baseball team less likely to take a gamble on Bo. In Bo's mind, given all the factors, he has to feel football would be the wiser choice."

If Bo was now leaning toward football, he still wasn't saying so. In fact, the end of his baseball season made it easier for him to avoid the media crush and relax a bit. Even Coach Baird noticed that a few days away from the field made Bo "the most relaxed and happiest I've seen him since I've been at Auburn."

"Everybody needs a rest," Bo said. "I had been spreading myself too thin. I wanted to get away from the media and get myself back."

As the April 29 NFL draft day approached, Bo realized it was time to get himself some high-powered representation. That a marquee name like Bo Jackson didn't already have an agent was surprising since agents are a breed famous for going after top college athletes as if they were a fumbled football. Up until early June, Bo was being advised by a man named Frelon Abbott, Jr., a family friend and Auburn booster. But now, with negotiations over big-money deals and complicated contracts on the horizon, the future pro needed pros to do his bidding in the bidding wars. Abbott advised Jackson to seek out a law firm instead of an agent, and Bo agreed with the strategy.

"I looked at a bunch of people," Bo explained to *Busi-*

ness Alabama magazine, "and how their agents represent them, and what they do for them. To me an agent is a waste of time and money, because you pay him to handle your business and he goes out and hires a lawyer to work for him. So I decided to bypass the agent and go straight to the lawyer."

Bo hired the Mobile, Alabama, law firm of Miller, Hamilton, Snider, & Odom to carry the ball—and bats—for him, even though the group had never handled sports law. With the NFL draft just a few weeks away, the baseball draft a month after that, and their client interested in pursuing talks with both sports, the firm's junior partners, Tom Zieman (who would handle football negotiations) and Richard Woods (who would talk baseball), gave themselves cram courses in sports law and contracts.

"We had to learn buzzwords like skill guarantees, injury guarantees, annuities, and signing, reporting, and performance bonuses," Zieman recalled. "And we had to learn about the difference between the football and baseball markets, and the different rules in each sport. For instance, we found out we could talk to Tampa Bay about contracts before their draft, but we couldn't talk to any baseball teams about money until after theirs."

While Zieman flew to Tampa to talk big bucks with the Bucs, Jackson went to California with Woods for a promotional appearance. Bo stopped by Anaheim Stadium to watch the Angels play and spent some time chatting with another Jackson—Reggie, his long-time baseball idol, who was wrapping up his playing career. Reggie told Bo that he'd heard glowing scouting reports about him and that he could write his own ticket if he became a baseball star. The straw that stirred the drink told the kid who chewed on straws that he could be the next—who else?—Reggie Jackson.

Speculation about Bo and the Angels swirled almost immediately, especially since California would have five picks in the first round of the June draft. Would they draft Bo a second year in a row? Privately, it was clear that they were interested. Publicly, the Angels remained as noncommittal as Bo.

"With five first-rounders, it's a risk we can take," admitted Angels scouting director Larry Himes. "But I don't think we would even draft Bo unless he makes a commitment that he's interested in playing baseball."

As preliminary contract talks began with Tampa Bay, another party entered the Bo Jackson sweepstakes a week before the NFL draft—the USFL's Birmingham Stallions. Although the young league was on such shaky financial ground that the Stallions were forced to borrow money the previous year, it was hoping to win a $1.3 billion antitrust suit against the NFL. A ruling in their favor would provide the Stallions with enough money to make Jackson take them seriously.

"We're trying to make Birmingham the capital for professional football as well as college football," said Stallions board chairman Harold Ripps as he stood beside Bo at an April 23 press conference. "We'd like to talk Bo into playing for us and doing what he does best in his hometown."

Nobody thought Jackson would want to play in the USFL, but the offer made by the Stallions certainly didn't hurt Bo's bargaining position with the other two major sports leagues. When asked if Birmingham had a shot at him, Bo played it coy with the media. "I'm in the supermarket shopping," he told the press in Birmingham, "and I'm going to sample all the fruit before I pick one. All my doors are open. The reason I'm waiting until the baseball draft is I want to give everybody a fair shot. Once I make my decision on what I want to do, I don't want the rest of the world to say, 'He didn't give us a chance.' "

For two days in late April, Bo Jackson would be the center of attention from McAdory to Manhattan. On Sunday the twenty-eighth, the day before the NFL draft, it was "Bo Jackson Day" in his hometown and at his former high school. Bo's lawyers had wanted him in New York to accommodate media interview requests, but Bo wasn't going to miss his day of honor for the world. More than 10,000 people attended a parade—led by Auburn University cheerleaders—that began in Bessemer and ended at McAdory. In the high-school auditorium, with a high-school band playing and the crowd cheering, the school retired Bo's number, 40.

"Four years ago I told people," said Bill Legg, the athletic director for Jefferson County, "that Bo Jackson was the greatest athlete ever to come through our area's schools. I'm happy to say he made a prophet out of me. Like the astronauts, Bo Jackson is made of the right stuff."

As tumultuous cheers filled the hall, Bo walked to the podium, visibly impressed by the outpouring of love and affection. "It's a great feeling to be home," he told his fans. "I've come a long way, and the road is still long. I'm looking forward to every step I take." In a light moment, he added, "I'm at the point now where I've got lawyers. They work for me. Four years ago, the only lawyer I knew was Perry Mason."

Then, getting serious again, Bo decided to impart some life lessons.

"Criticism will always be there," he told the assemblage, consisting mostly of high-school students. "Use criticism as fuel for your fire. . . . I know what Bo is. Bo's a man."

The next morning, Bo was *the* man. At a little after

nine A.M., in a banquet hall of New York's Marriott Marquis Hotel, NFL Commissioner Pete Rozelle stepped to a podium with a card indicating the first selection of the 1986 NFL draft. Rozelle, who always liked to milk the drama during these announcements, said slowly, "First pick, first round, Tampa Bay . . ."

The hundreds of draftniks sitting in the gallery began chanting, *"Bo! Bo! Bo! Bo!"*

Then Rozelle said the words: ". . . Bo Jackson, running back, Auburn University."

But Bo's moment of glory was tempered somewhat by the fact that negotiations with the Buccaneers were going slower than the last two minutes of a football game. Tampa's owner Hugh Culverhouse did not attend the draft, as is the custom, and nobody held up an orange Tampa Bay jersey with Bo's name and number on it. As long as Bo was going to remain uncommitted until the baseball draft, Hugh Culverhouse was not going to talk serious money with Bo's lawyers. In fact, the weekend before the draft, Culverhouse had told Zieman that the Bucs wouldn't make an offer unless Bo *asked* to play with his team. Tampa even entertained offers from other teams—San Francisco 49ers, Washington Redskins, New England Patriots, and Kansas City Chiefs—for their number-one pick, but the trade demands of the Bucs made a deal impossible.

"That was a strange way to deal with a Heisman Trophy winner," Zieman said in *Business Alabama* later that year. "Culverhouse is a businessman who negotiates from a position of strength, and he clearly didn't have that with Bo, because Bo Jackson isn't driven by the dollar: He's driven by what Bo Jackson wants to do."

By mid-May talks between Tampa and Jackson's lawyers hadn't progressed, and by then two more baseball teams said they were interested in drafting Bo. The To-

ronto Blue Jays and the 1985 World Champion Kansas
City Royals told Richard Woods that Bo had superstar potential. The Royals's interest was intriguing, but not surprising, since Hal Baird, Bo's baseball coach at Auburn,
had played in the Kansas City organization, and Ken Gonzales, a Royals scout based in Alabama, had been watching
Bo since high school. Kansas City's scouting director Art
Stewart had long considered Jackson a franchise-type
player based on the scouting reports he had gotten from
Gonzales and Dick Egan of the Major League Scouting
Bureau. Gonzales had rated Jackson's potential at 71 on a
system where anything over 70 was a superstar. Egan rated
Jackson at 75.5, at that time the highest overall rating in
the 15-year history of the bureau. Stewart thought Jackson
could be another Mickey Mantle or Willie Mays.

Woods and Zieman told the Royals that they were not
expecting a baseball team to match a football offer dollar
for dollar. Bo was genuinely interested in baseball, the
lawyers said, but to make it a viable option the sport would
have to offer more than what usually went to a number-
one pick (which was in the neighborhood of $100,000 a
year). The Royals said they understood the lawyers' position on the money, but still needed some assurances that
Bo wanted to play baseball. Even though none of the teams
would pick Jackson in the first round, they weren't about
to gamble any pick on Bo if he wasn't signable.

"The neatest trick we had to turn," one of the lawyers
recalled, "was to convince a major-league baseball organization that Bo was serious about the game, without rep-
resenting that he definitely would play. Because that was
something we had the power to do, and would have been
lying if we'd done so."

The weekend before the baseball draft, Jackson and his
lawyers met in Atlanta to mull over all the options. It was

at that meeting when Bo told Zieman and Woods that, as far as baseball was concerned, he wasn't interested in Toronto or California. So on the Sunday night before the draft, Zieman called Royals general manager John Schuerholz and told him that Bo's preference was Kansas City. Schuerholz asked Bo if he liked baseball as much as football, and Bo replied, "I've played baseball since I was nine years old. I have learned to love football as much as baseball, not the other way around."

John Schuerholz lay awake all that night thinking about whether he would gamble on drafting Bo Jackson and, just as importantly, *when* he would do it. The baseball world found out those answers the next day. When Schuerholz still saw Jackson's name on the board in the fourth round—Toronto and California had obviously lost interest—he made Bo the one hundred fourth player to be drafted in 1986.

"We didn't draft Bo Jackson in the fourth round to attract attention," Schuerholz told the media. "We feel he has the potential to be an outstanding baseball player and he has some interest in playing baseball. How much remains to be seen. We felt like where we drafted him we could take a calculated gamble, and we did. We don't feel we've harmed ourselves in the drafting process at all in selecting Bo."

When Bo heard the news, he was, as Richard Woods put it, "on cloud nine." And when Woods saw just how happy Bo was, the lawyer finally realized his client had always been more interested in baseball. Of course, for negotiation purposes, he couldn't let on that Bo "was thrilled to be drafted by the World Champion Kansas City Royals."

Not so thrilled about the news were the Tampa Bay Buccaneers, although owner Hugh Culverhouse feigned indifference. He claimed his team's position wasn't affected by the baseball draft. He reiterated his promise to make Jackson "the highest-paid rookie to ever enter the National Football League," which would mean topping the five-year, $5 million contract John Elway received from the Denver Broncos in 1983.

In negotiations, however, Culverhouse played hardball with pro-football's hottest prospect. While the press speculated that the owner was offering Jackson over $7 million for five years, the actual offer to Bo was for approximately $4 million over five years, including a $1.5 million signing bonus. The discrepancy between rumor and fact wasn't surprising to those who knew Culverhouse. The Bucs's owner was a force on the NFL's Management Council and had a reputation for wanting to hold the line on salaries. Culverhouse was not only breaking his promise on the salary; when he made his offer on June 14, he told the media that it would be withdrawn if Jackson didn't accept it within the next week. Two days later, Bo's lawyer asked the Bucs to raise their yearly guaranteed money package. Culverhouse said no-go, Bo.

Kansas City, on the other hand, was courting Bo and his lawyers in Royal style. They were flown to Memphis in co-owner Ewing Kauffman's private jet and began negotiations with co-owner Avron Fogelman. Kansas City's offer was for $850,000 over three years, with $200,000 paid in the first year. The Royals also wanted termination clauses in the contract in case Bo wanted to quit baseball for football. If he left baseball after the first year, he would have to pay back the $200,000. After the second year, he'd have to return 50 percent.

But although the offer made by the Royals was considerably less than Tampa's, the team was offering other perks. Fogelman offered to establish a $10,000 scholarship

Bo Jackson was one of the most awesome combinations of running speed and power in college football history. During four years at Auburn University, Jackson set school records in yards gained (4,303) and touchdowns (43).

Bo scampers for a 67-yard touchdown against Georgia during his 1985 senior year. His season totals of 1,786 yards and 17 touchdowns were not only Auburn records, but were enough to earn him the coveted Heisman Trophy. *(Photos courtesy of Auburn University)*

Bo's not the one plucking the guitar in this photo taken before the 1984 Sugar Bowl, but he sure knew diddley against Michigan, rushing for 130 yards and leading the cheers (below) in Auburn's 9–7 Bowl victory. *(Photos courtesy of Auburn University)*

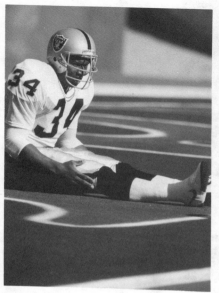

Bo became a two-sport pro in 1987 when he signed with the Los Angeles Raiders. Though his football season didn't start until the baseball schedule ended, Bo immediately electrified football fans with his explosive runs, including one memorable 91-yard Monday Night scamper against the Seattle Seahawks. *(Photos by Bryan Yablonsky)*

By 1988, Bo was hitting and running his way to baseball superstardom. Jackson's .246 average, 25 home runs and 27 stolen bases provided glimpses of even greater achievements to come.
(Photos by Bryan Yablonsky)

At the plate, Bo has been the epitome of power since he joined the Kansas City Royals late during the 1986 season. Although he has become one of the major league strikeout leaders, he averaged 27 home runs per year between 1987 and '89. Some of Jackson's blasts in Kansas City have been among the longest ever hit at Royals Stadium.
(Photos by Michael Ponzini)

As Auburn's star baseball player in 1985, Bo made major league scouts drool, as he batted .401 with 17 homers and 43 runs batted in. *(Photo courtesy of Auburn University)*

In three NFL seasons (all shortened by baseball), Jackson has established himself as one of football's great running backs. Bo has run for 2,084 total yards and is the only player in pro football history ever to run for two 90-yard touchdowns in a career. *(Photos by Bryan Yablonsky)*

People began calling Bo "America's Greatest Athlete" after his incredible performance in the 1989 All-Star Game. His first-inning home run off Rick Reuschel (Bo also singled, stole a base, and made a great catch in the outfield) ignited a 5–3 American League victory and earned Bo the game's Most Valuable Player Award. Jackson finished the '89 campaign with 32 homers and 105 RBIs. *(Photo courtesy Kansas City Royals)*

fund at Auburn in Jackson's name, pay the rest of his college tuition, and to set Bo up as a volunteer counselor in a program that provided tuition at junior colleges for minority students. The Royals, aware of Bo's dislike for practice, also reminded him that in baseball he'd play every day instead of practicing six days to play one. This soft-sell, as opposed to Tampa Bay's hard line, appealed to Jackson and his lawyers. "The Royals had a genuine interest in Bo," Zieman recalled, "and went out of their way to entice him from football."

Bo was now ready to sign with Kansas City. The only stumbling block was Woods's insistence on making his client a "million-dollar player." Kansas City balked, saying they didn't want to throw their team's salary structure out of whack. After some more haggling and redefining of certain aspects of the contract, the total offer made by the Royals came to $1,066,000 over three years. Woods showed Bo the contract and, without reading it, Jackson said, "If it's good enough for you, it's good enough for me."

Later Ewing Kauffman would say, "Football guaranteed him two million dollars; we guaranteed him two hundred thousand. I think it shows his self-confidence and character. In the long run, he'll make more money from us than football, and he'll be able to walk when he's fifty."

At the two June 21 press conferences—one in Birmingham and the other in Kansas City—announcing the deal, the burning question was: Why hadn't Bo chosen the more lucrative football offer?

The answer, he said, was simple. "I could have played football," Bo said in Birmingham. "I could have signed a contract and become an instant millionaire. You all can say anything, but I'm trying to make a living. This is the first day of summer, and summer's a time for baseball and I'm ready to go. This is what Bo wants to do the rest of his life. I've never had my legs cut on, and I never plan to go to the hospital.''

Still, Bo admitted that he had struggled with the decision for weeks before signing with Kansas City.

"I'd wake up in the morning and be leaning toward something different every day," he said at Royals Stadium. "Finally, I asked myself, 'What am I going to do?' The answer to that question is standing right here. And you know what? I probably wouldn't be standing here if it weren't for Reggie Jackson."

Some writers asked Reggie for his insights into the man who could became another baseball superstar named Jackson. Reggie talked about how impressed he was with Bo's confidence with who he was and where he was going. "The man's a killer," Reggie observed. "You see that in the bridge of a man's nose. That's where you see the eyes, what's going on inside a man, what he's feeling and thinking, how tough he is. And I'm telling you, Bo Jackson is tough.''

After all the questions had been asked and answered, Reggie, the Royals, the writers—everybody—went to the batting cage to watch how tough Bo Jackson would be on a baseball. As he blasted pitch after batting-practice pitch far beyond the outfield fence at Royals Stadium, the amazed observers traded thoughts and insights about this future star.

"When you get a chance to get a helluva player," Royals superstar George Brett said, "you've got to do it. The players here are excited to be a teammate of Bo's."

And Royals second baseman Frank White added, "Baseball needs people like Bo. If he can do the things that are anticipated he can do, it's going to help everybody. That's the bottom line."

"It would have been easy to write him off and say he's

going to play football," said proud scout Kenny Gonzales, as he watched Bo stinging line drives. Gonzales had traveled hundreds of miles following Jackson since Bo had been a high-school senior. "I remember one scout coming up to me during his senior year at Auburn and saying, 'He's not going to play baseball. You're wasting your time. But for argument's sake, let's say he does. He'll never make it. He'll struggle in the rookie league and it'll take him two years to get out of there.' Another scout told me, 'He's got all the right muscles, but in all the wrong places.' Everyone had some excuse why they didn't draft Bo."

It seems some baseball purists just can't accept a player who possesses so much talent, yet has so little classical training. They become uncomfortable when they see somebody so easily taking the mystery out of their game. Tommy Jones, the manager of the Memphis Chicks Double-A team, which would be Bo's first professional stop, was one of those baseball purists. He looked at the man hitting in the Kansas City batting cage and saw a baseball player whose skills were crude and awkward and unrefined. Then he saw Bo Jackson hit a ball that seemed to travel from Kansas City to St. Louis along Interstate 70.

"I swear," Tommy Jones said, "I'm looking at Ted Williams."

Bo
Knows
Failure

The fan walked out of Memphis's Chicks Stadium shaking his head and there was wonder in his eyes. "Was that the most unbelievable thing you've ever seen?" he asked some fellow fans. "It was almost a religious experience." The fan had just witnessed the Bo Jackson legend. He had seen powerful Bo from Kansas City, Mo, blast 9 of his first 25 professional batting-practice pitches over a fence far, far away.

"It was as awesome a display as I've ever seen for the first time seeing a guy," said Ken Berry, the minor-league hitting instructor for the Royals. "The best part was that he was hitting the low pitch well. You don't last long here if you don't hit the low ball."

You also don't stick around pro-baseball if you don't hit the curve ball, that devilish 80-plus m.p.h. pitch that dances down and away from a batter as if repelled by wood. Could Bo Jackson pulverize the curve, too? That's what the writers covering Bo's first BP session wanted to know.

"You are the ones with the doubts," Jackson told the scribes. "I think some people see Bo Jackson as the type of guy that can't be beat. That's not true. I'm human just like everybody else. At this point I want to be treated like one of the players, not like 'Bo Jackson the-Heisman-Trophy-winner.' I'm here to play ball and let things work themselves out. I know I'm a long way from being ready.''

But everybody was certainly ready for Bo. His Memphis debut on Monday evening, June 30, had generated 25,000 ticket requests for a stadium that seated only 9,582. And more than 175 media members requested credentials, including the ABC television network, which would be breaking into its "Monday Night Baseball" coverage to show Bo's first pro at-bats. That's star power.

The lineup of Chicks manager Tommy Jones (who Jackson referred to as "my head coach" at a press conference that day) had Bo penciled in as the designated hitter, batting seventh. Like everyone else, Jones was impressed by Bo's athletic prowess, but the manager was skeptical about Jackson's baseball skills. "He really had no feel for how the professional game was played," Jones recalled. "He looked like a football player in a baseball uniform. Defensively, when he reported to Memphis, he was no more prepared to play outfield than some guy who stepped off a beer-league softball diamond.''

As Bo stood in the on-deck circle in the first inning, he experienced a feeling that for him was quite rare—jittery nerves. His large hands shook as he unwrapped some pieces of chewing gum. He hadn't felt quite that nervous since the last seconds before the Heisman Trophy winner was announced. When his name was called this time, Bo walked to the plate while just over 7,000 fans (many didn't show up thinking they wouldn't find seats) gave him a standing ovation. The first pitch from Columbus Astros pitcher Mitch Cook was a ball. Then, with the count 2–1, Bo swung and sent a grounder up the middle for a base hit and an RBI. "Goodness gracious," Chicks President,

George Lapides, said, "the only thing better would have been a home run."

There would be no home runs—or any other hits, for that matter—for Bo Jackson that night. In fact, during his first two weeks with the Chicks, Bo's offense was nonexistent. Jackson had always taken pride in playing on levels higher than his age. But against these seasoned pro pitchers, he looked like a Little Leaguer. In his first 12 games— 9 as a right fielder and 3 as a designated hitter—Jackson got only 4 hits in 45 at-bats, for a .089 average. Even worse, he had struck out 21 times. Southern League pitchers were saying that Bo was overmatched, that he was having trouble with the curve ball and the fast ball inside. Some suggested Bo would be better off in a rookie league. And the Royals, whose scouts were watching Bo's every move, began second-guessing their decision to start Jackson as high as Double-A ball. They called manager Tommy Jones every day and decided to be patient with their highly paid prodigy.

"He's going to play nine innings of every single game and get his at-bats," Jones said. "I don't want to rob him of any experience he's getting right now. Our won-loss record is secondary to the development of the prospects on this team."

"We'll give him about one hundred fifty, two hundred at-bats, until about the end of August," said hitting instructor Ken Berry. "If he's still striking out three or four times a game on curve balls, we have a problem. But I don't anticipate a problem. I've been told my body will be in the river if I mess with him."

Though Bo was experiencing his first very public failure, he remained even-tempered through the adversity. He didn't even let the long bus trips get him down. "He's handling it like a fifteen-year veteran," said his impressed manager. Bo arrived at the ball park at noon for night games and took hours of batting practice. Pitching coach Rich Dubee threw sliders, curves, and change-ups, and Bo worked on hitting the pitches to various parts of the field. He also practiced getting his hands out quickly to pull the inside fast ball. He wanted to think about nothing but baseball before games, so he spoke with the media only after games. He told the writers he wasn't worried about the slump. He knew he'd come out of it. After all, who knew Bo better than Bo?

"I've always gotten off to a slow start in baseball," Bo explained. "It's always taken a good month for me to get my feet on the ground. I don't care if I go 2-for-200, I'm going to have confidence. I'm the type guy that won't let you beat me."

Bo wasn't about to take a month before beating up on Southern League pitchers. On July 12, a two-hit game against Charlotte ignited a Jackson hitting explosion. The next day, he celebrated the birth of his son Garrett (though he and Linda still weren't married) with his first professional homer, a three-run blast hit so high above the light standards that the left fielder couldn't see the ball in the dark. Over 8 games, including those 2, he batted .423 with 11 hits in 26 at-bats, 3 triples, 3 homers, 11 RBI's, and 7 runs scored, statistics that earned him Southern League Player of the Week honors. In the middle of this spectacular batting surge, Bo won a game against Greenville with a grand slam that was measured at 550 feet.

Bo's streak became the talk of the league and he brought out fans and media wherever he played. When the Chicks played in Huntsville, 11,583 fans attended, constituting the second-largest crowd in the stadium's two-year history. At Charlotte, the attendance was almost 11,000 for a four-game series, compared to almost 5,000 the previous four games. In Greenville and Chattanooga, 10,000 more fans came out to watch four games with the Chicks than had seen the four games before Memphis was in town. And everywhere the team went on the road, there turned out as big a media crush as one might see in New York or Los Angeles. "He's sure stimulated some interest," said league president Jimmy Bragan in an understatement. "I can't recall any other players that had the same effect on attendance."

After his horrendous 4-for-45 start with the Chicks, Bo batted .338 (47-for-139) over the last 40 games and hit safely in 40 of his last 48. When pitchers threw curve balls outside, Bo slapped them to right field. When they threw fast balls inside, Bo would pull them to left field—that is, when they weren't sawing the bat off in his hands. The negatives? He struck out 81 times and hadn't worked out all the kinks in his defense and base running. He was still erratic in the field, making seven errors, and despite his great speed, he was thrown out in his first five steal attempts. Even with the flaws, Jackson was named by *Baseball America* as the number-one major-league prospect from the Southern League in 1986.

"A lot of people thought he wouldn't make it in this league," Tommy Jones said, "and Bo's proved them wrong. He progressed very, very quickly. You make a few suggestions here and there, and he'll put them into the game that night." The Royals were so pleased with Bo's turnaround at Memphis that they brought him to Kansas City. When the rosters expanded to 40 on September 1, the Royals were out of the pennant race so Jackson could move right into the lineup and strut his stuff without much pressure. He would be the first player in Royals history to go from the college campus to the big club in the same season. Tommy Jones joked that Jackson had "probably played the fewest games of anyone to suit up in the majors since 1951, when Bill Veeck played that midget [Eddie Gaedel]."

Bo made his major-league debut on September 2, and he revved up Royals fans in his first at-bat. Future Hall of Fame left-hander Steve Carlton was on the mound for the Chicago White Sox. Jackson worked the count to 2–2 and then Carlton threw a slider that hung in Bo's power zone. Bo turned on the pitch and launched it down the left-field line, somewhere above the 90-foot high foul pole. The ball traveled about 425 feet. The only problem was that it went foul. When the call was made, Bo had already gotten to second base and milked a standing ovation as he walked back to the plate. Not many players can send a crowd into a frenzy on a foul ball. Two pitches later, Bo tapped a grounder between first and second base and beat Carlton to the bag easily for a major-league hit in his first at-bat. Later in the game, Bo hit a ground ball that was so hard, only his sprinter's speed prevented it from being turned into a triple play. Scouts sitting behind the plate timing Bo from home to first did double-takes when they saw stopwatches that read three-point-six-six seconds. And Royals veteran Jorge Orta noticed that Bo "goes across the first-base bag like he's breaking the tape in the sixty-yard dash."

It had been only one game, but after it was over, Royals executives were dreaming wonderful baseball dreams. Besides, where else but in dreams does a career baseball man see a player with such an overwhelming combination of speed and power? "He's crude and he's green," Royals manager Mike Ferraro said. "But I can only wonder what he'll be like in three years with all that raw talent."

Al Stewart, the Royals scouting director, said, "In thirty-five years, I've never seen a player with that kind of athletic ability come into this game. I don't even think the media fully realize it yet—we're talking about one of the finest athletes of our time. He's going to be something else.''

But it wasn't time to open up a wing in the Hall of Fame just yet. Sure, Bo had a few more special games. In his fifth start, he had a four-hit game, three of which were legged-out ground balls. And on September 14, Bo hit his first major-league homer, a 475-foot blast to left center field off Seattle's Mike Moore that Kansas City officials said was the longest homer ever hit at Royals Stadium. After that game, his seventh, Bo's average stood at .333 (9-for-27). But over his last 18 games, Bo went just 8-for-55 and finished the season at a disappointing .207.

Some Royals players claimed Bo's slump was the result of poor work habits. He would miss extra batting practices and sit on the bench during fielding warm-ups. Some people thought Bo's mind had drifted toward football, especially since he had only until October 1 to break his contract, and Tampa Bay owner Hugh Culverhouse had made Jackson another offer to play for the Bucs. This time the owner was offering real estate with the big-money package. Bo still wasn't interested.

''There's nothing about football that I really miss,'' Bo insisted when the media pressed him on the matter. ''I don't know why it's so hard for people to understand that. For the last six years, it was my life. I enjoyed it and I reminisce over it, but I don't miss it. If people still don't understand why I turned down the money from Tampa, that's their problem. Bo's happy. Bo's doing what Bo wants to do. That's all that matters.''

But what also mattered to Bo was refining his raw baseball skills and silencing those whispers about his work habits. With fall football out of his life for the first time in eight years, Bo spent three weeks in the Florida Instructional League, then a few more weeks working out on the Auburn campus. He spent hours each day taking batting practice, positioning in the outfield on base hits, and learning how to chase fly balls. Bo's dedication in these sessions astounded his former coach, Hal Baird, who knew how much Jackson disliked practice. "This winter I saw that Bo had completely committed himself to baseball greatness," Baird said.

Bo also committed himself to some serious soul-searching. He knew he could have worked harder after his September call-up. Bo began to know guilt and humility. "I'm not ashamed to say it," he told the *Kansas City Star* that winter, "but I never had to work hard at anything until I signed with the Royals. Everything before that had come so easy and so simple. I can stand back now and see where I should have shown a little more hustle last year.

"As for my hitting, well, I'd watch George Brett and Willie Wilson take batting practice and they'd just swat at the balls, so I figured I could do the same thing. That was a mistake. I forgot that they had worked for years to reach that level, that they had worked hard in spring training just for that year."

Bo knew that to avoid the minors in 1987, he'd have to, as he put it, "work my butt off this spring, which I'm not used to." He was determined to outhustle, outwork, and outsweat everybody at training camp and force the Royals to keep him with the major-league club.

The hard work paid off. In the spring exhibition games, Bo batted .273 with 3 homers and 11 RBI's, and his fine defensive play made George Brett ask rhetorically, "Who says Bo doesn't belong?"

But even if general manager John Schuerholz thought Bo still needed some minor-league seasoning, he couldn't act on it. Royals co-owner Avron Fogelman insisted that Schuerholz ask Jackson if he thought he was ready for the majors. Naturally, Bo wasn't about to opt for the bad food, long bus trips, and dingy motels that came with life in the minors. So some players were juggled around and Bo Jackson became the 1987 Royals opening-day left fielder.

For a while the Royals were happy Bo had forced their hand. In four games between April 10 and 14, Jackson went 12-for-16 with 12 RBI's, including a 4-hit, 2-home-run, seven-RBI night against the Detroit Tigers. One of the homers was a broken-bat grand slam job that sailed over the center field fence at Royals Stadium. But Bo was still Dr. Jekyll and Mr. Whiff at the plate. Before the four-game hot streak, he struck out 7 times in his first 13 at-bats, and after the streak he whiffed 20 times in 10 games, including a 5-strikeout night (only the twenty-fifth player ever to do that) against the New York Yankees. By the end of April, Bo was striking out once every 2.91 times at bat.

But when Bo was making contact, he was hitting the heck out of the horsehide. His April average was .324 with 4 home runs and 15 RBI's. Royals designated hitter and part-time batting instructor Hal McRae was especially impressed, both with Bo's hitting style and his ability to bounce back after bad games.

"He's got the greatest bat speed I've ever seen," McRae told *Sports Illustrated,* which by May was already pushing Jackson as a Rookie of the Year candidate. "And lifting his front leg is one of many good things he does naturally. It gives him a better look at the ball and lets him wait a little longer, because his upper body doesn't move forward. He can learn more by doing than from instruction because he's good at controlling himself. If he loses it, he can gather himself for his next at-bat. You can't teach that, any more than you can teach bat speed.''

While Bo was tearing up the American League that April, National Football League teams were preparing for the end-of-the-month draft of college players. A few NFL teams called Bo's agent, Richard Woods, asking what Bo would do if they drafted him. Woods told them all the same thing—that Bo was happy with baseball and was committed to the Royals. The assumption had always been that any football team drafting Bo would want him to give up baseball for good. But Al Davis, the maverick owner of the Los Angeles Raiders, had another idea.

Davis had not been one of the owners who called Woods, but when the Raiders had their turn in the seventh round of the draft, he stunned the entire sports world with these words: ''The Raiders select Bo Jackson, running back, from Auburn.'' Davis never thought he was wasting a pick because he had something up his sleeve. He wouldn't make Bo choose between baseball and football; he would take Bo on to the Raiders after the baseball season was over. Al Davis would take a guy who could run a 4.1-second, 40-yard dash any day, even if it meant having him for only half a season.

''I don't think there is any other athlete who could play baseball and football at the professional level except Bo Jackson,'' Davis said. ''He is that great. We feel he can do it. We want him to look at it as a challenge to prove he is the greatest.''

Would Bo take Davis up on his offer? Would he play both baseball and football during the same season? Though he was flattered and amused by it all, Jackson kept insisting that he'd had it with football. But as the days passed, and Bo realized playing two sports might be a realistic option, he became more intrigued and excited about the idea. In late June, Bo told Woods to contact Davis, and negotiations began about a deal that would make Bo Jackson a pro-football player. About two weeks later, on July 11, the Royals received news that they never wanted to hear—Bo Jackson would be signing a contract with the Raiders.

"I'm thinking about adding another hobby to my off-season curriculum, and that's all it would be," Jackson said at a news conference in Toronto. "I have to do my job with the Kansas City Royals before I do anything else. Whatever comes after baseball season is a hobby for Bo Jackson, just like fishing and hunting."

Two of Bo's old coaches were not among those surprised by their former player's decision. "I think he did it," said Dick Atchison, "because Bo can't concentrate on any one thing for twelve months at a time."

And Pat Dye said, "If there's one thing I've learned from my association with Bo Jackson, it's that you never, ever underestimate what he can do. I think that playing baseball and football would be more than most people could handle. But if there's anybody in the country—no, the world—that can do it, it's Bo. One thing for sure, there's no doubt that he can play football."

The Royals organization was now faced with a Solomon-like decision. Privately, they were disappointed, but publicly they put a good face on the situation. Avron Fogelman never considered giving Jackson an ultimatum to choose one sport or the other. The co-owner understood Bo's desire to attempt playing two sports. "The Royals think it is very important to do whatever is in Bo's best interests," Fogelman said. "He thought it was the opportune time to try to do something that no one else has ever done, and we wish Bo a lot of success."

General Manager John Schuerholz was skeptical about

Bo's ability to pull off the feat: "The question is: Can anybody withstand the physical stress of football playing for a limited amount of games and maintain the strength and agility of one hundred sixty-two games of baseball? I just don't know."

Bo's teammates on the Royals weren't quite so understanding. When Bo made his announcement, they had just lost their fifth straight game of a tough road trip. They joined much of the sports media in blasting Bo's use of the word *hobby* when referring to football and thought the front office was favoring Bo over the rest of the team. Center fielder Willie Wilson was especially angry about the whole affair. "You think it's a hobby for Lawrence Taylor when he tackles you?" Wilson asked. "I'm mad, and this team's mad—not at Bo as much as the front office. We've got guys here ten years, twelve years, but now there's a guy been here three months and saying how he wants things done.

"The front office hasn't got any respect for us, so why should we respect them? Tell them to take that to the bank. I don't give a damn. I'm so mad I can't stand it. If they don't like what I said, they can release me. Trade me, I don't care. I get paid for the next forty years, anyway."

Second baseman Frank White's comment was even more damning of the Royals front office. "The game's not about winning anymore. It's about putting a show on the field. The key is putting people in the stands, and it's obvious that's all our management cares about."

"Bo's not gone," said rookie third baseman Kevin Seitzer, "but you get the feeling he's run out on us."

And right fielder Danny Tartabull, Bo's closest friend on the Royals, added, "I hope all this doesn't distract the other players and destroy the team."

When the Royals returned to Kansas City, the fans

booed Bo and threw tiny footballs at him with the slogan that read IT'S A HOBBY. Jackson won back their affection briefly when he made two spectacular fielding plays in the July 17 game against Baltimore. But Bo didn't help his case with the fans after the game when he called those who were booing "jealous" and added, "They don't have anything else better to do. I have nothing negative to say about the fans. A person who can't take criticism is a fool. And I can't tell you what the person who gives criticism is called. It's X-rated."

The same term could be used to describe Jackson's second half. Danny Tartabull's worst fears were realized. At the time of Bo's football announcement, at the All-Star break, he was hitting .253 with 37 runs, 13 doubles, 18 homers, and 45 RBI's in 79 games. After the announcement, he had only 4 hits in his next 25 at-bats and struck out 25 times. By the end of July, Jackson was being taken out for pinch hitters, and during August he was benched. In September, the Minnesota Twins moved ahead of the Royals into first place. Manager Billy Gardner was fired and replaced by John Wathan. Kansas City fans (who constantly booed Bo), the media (which was still calling Bo "selfish" for his football decision), and some Kansas City players ("It was a major distraction that ruined our season," said Tartabull) blamed Bo for the second-half collapse of the Royals. However, George Brett defended Jackson, saying, "How could Bo lose the race for us when he played so little?"

After the football announcement, Bo batted just .193 (23-for-119) with 9 runs, 4 doubles, 4 homers, 8 RBI's, and 46 strikeouts in 37 games. (He led the team in strikeouts with 158.) For the year, Bo set a Royals rookie record with 22 home runs, but he batted just .235 with only 53 RBI's. Defensively, almost every fly ball hit his way during the second half had become an adventure. "He just wasn't the same player, that's all there is to it," John Schuerholz said. For Bo, the early season success and euphoria had turned into failure, frustration, and despair. Once the year ended, Bo revealed some of the hurt and anguish he felt when the baseball season was taken away from him. They were feelings he had expressed only to Linda, whom he'd married in September, when he was at his lowest point of the season.

"You know that [anti-perspirant] commercial? 'Never let anyone see you sweat'?" he told the *Kansas City Star*. "Well, that was me. No one knew what I was feeling. But I'll be honest with you, there were times I was bitter. There were days when I just didn't want to come to the ball park. And there were other days when I just couldn't wait to leave.

"Everybody in the country knows why Bo was sitting on the bench. And it wasn't because of the errors. And it wasn't because I wasn't hitting the ball. People have told me the Royals are testing me. Well, I'm a strong person. I was mentally tough long before I got to this sport."

But the question persisted. Would Bo come back to the Royals in 1988 and play out the third year of his contract?

"You can never expect my next move until I tell you about it," said Bo, being typically mysterious. "People ask me all the time, and I just say, 'Come to spring training and find out.' I know in my own mind, but I'm not saying. And I'm not going to make any announcements; I've already made enough announcements in my lifetime."

John Schuerholz assumed that Bo would be back in 1988. "He can still be one of the all-time greats, especially if he concentrates on baseball," the GM said. But baseball would have to wait until February. Now it was time for Bo to concentrate on his "hobby."

Bo
Knows
Football—Again

In a 1989 *TV Guide* article, Al Davis was asked for the umpteenth time since signing Bo Jackson in 1987 why he could accept him as just a part-time Raider running back. And for the umpteenth time Davis responded with a variation of the same answer he'd been giving for two years. "When there is a great player who can make a contribution in both sports," he said, "you have to give him the opportunity to do it. I signed this guy as an adjunct. He is a special force designed to pick us up through the last ten or so games. Where can you get talent like that for nothing except money?"

But by the end of the '89 season, Davis must have been secretly wishing that he had talked Bo Jackson into making the Raiders his sole obsession back in '87. Jackson had picked the Raiders up, all right—the team had overcome a 2-3 pre-Bo start and was 8–7 in the AFC West heading into the season finale against the New York Giants—but even with a last-game victory, only a miracle would get them into the playoffs. Those three early season losses— by five to Kansas City, ten to Denver, and four to Seattle— might have been victories with Bo in the backfield. So nobody could have blamed Davis if he thought that with Jackson around all season, a playoff spot would have already been clinched by week 16.

But to Al Davis, Bo was a bonus. Sure, he'd taken a calculated risk when he drafted Jackson in '87. But when Bo agreed to sign, Davis knew he'd be getting a better athlete than a whole bunch of number-seven draft picks combined. Anyway, even if Bo played only half a season, better he be wearing Raiders black and silver than the colors of one of the other 27 NFL teams.

As Bo prepared to report to the Raiders after his disappointing '87 baseball season, the sports media were still having a field day with all the "controversy" over his career decisions. There was speculation that the Raiders's players, some of whom had reputations for being the toughest and meanest in the sport, would be resentful of Bo's "hobby" comment and his large part-time salary. Some writers suggested that Marcus Allen, the superb halfback-Raider, would be jealous of Jackson. ("I haven't come here," Bo said, "to take someone's job or carry the team on my shoulders. I just want to be one of the players.") And just as with the baseball scribes, some football experts seemed to hope Bo would fail simply for having the audacity to attempt two professional sports careers. Jackson was still being vilified as everything from a crude opportunist to a traitor to baseball to a dilettante football player to a self-indulgent dunderhead.

It took a non-sports publication like *Life* magazine to put what sports people saw as "Bo's Folly" into perspective. The magazine bashed the myths that football was too complicated to play part-time and too grueling to play as a second sport. It quoted Pat Dye, saying: "You could fly Bo Jackson in on a jet right now, teach him five plays, show him which way to go, and on game day he'll make you look like a genius.''

As for football after baseball wearing Bo out, well, the late Alabama coach Bear Bryant once observed that a player's involvement in actual contact time during a football game was no more than six minutes. ''You're more likely to get bored to death than worn out,'' Bryant said.

Instead of criticizing Jackson's experiment, the magazine suggested the country should be celebrating the fact that ''an exceptional athlete will be trying something exceptional.''

Bo may not have been shocked or upset by all the criticism, but he was determined to prove the critics wrong. One just did not tell Bo Jackson he couldn't do something. ''I guess because I used the word *hobby*, which everybody took the wrong way, they used that as a match to start the fire,'' he told *Ebony* magazine. ''But I took all the flak, all the criticism, and all the 'He can't do its' and used it to fuel my fire.''

Jackson's '87 football season began in week seven after the three-week NFL players' strike. Raiders coach Tom Flores didn't think Bo was in ''football shape'' when he reported, so the coach decided Jackson would watch most of his first NFL game from the sidelines. Despite the long layoff after baseball, Bo still excited the crowd in New England when he finally got his hands on the ball with a little over 13 minutes left in the second quarter. He took quarterback Rusty Hilger's handoff and, finding no hole at the line of scrimmage, Bo bounced to the left sideline. As he began to accelerate downfield, Patriots Pro Bowl free safety Fred Marion attempted a tackle, but Bo's 230 punishing pounds were too much for the smaller Marion. Jackson bounced off him and another tackler and wasn't stopped until he'd gained 14 tough yards.

After the game, in which he gained 37 yards in 8 carries, Bo was asked what went through his mind during his first NFL run. "I was thinking, 'Don't fumble the frigging ball,' " he said.

Bo picked up the pace a bit in his next 2 games, running 12 times for 74 yards in a loss to the Vikings, and picking up another 48 yards in 8 carries in another defeat to Green Bay. Though he hadn't yet broken any long gainers, Bo was starting to run the way he did during his glory days at Auburn. Only now he was displaying a combination of power and agility that was rare among NFL running backs. "He could be the best in the league," Raiders defensive back Carl Lee observed. "He's big and fast, but a lot of guys are big and fast. What makes Bo different is that he can keep his balance even when two-hundred-fifty-pound linebackers are slamming into him. He won't go down."

Such ability was never more evident than during one play in the next game that the Raiders played, against the Denver Broncos. The Raiders had the ball on the Bronco 35-yard line when quarterback Mark Wilson handed off to Bo for a sweep to the right. As Bo approached the sideline, he saw Bronco defenders spinning off blocks and clogging holes. Instinctively, Bo stopped, turned, and took off for the left sideline. With Denver defenders in pursuit, Bo cut downfield, where he encountered cornerback Mike Hardin. Bo had already shown his speed and agility. Now was the time to exert power. He put down his head and bulldozed Hardin, knocking him out of the play. When Bo reached the five-yard line, three Broncos were ready to lasso him. This time, Bo took a page from his track days. Realizing he couldn't overpower three defenders, he leaped into the air and soared over them into the end zone. Bo Jackson's touchdown run against Denver was the highlight film of the week. Since the Seattle Seahawks would be next on the Raiders schedule, Seahawks coach Chuck Knox was more than interested in watching tapes of Bo's run against Denver. "That was a Hall of Fame play," raved Knox.

Jackson had scored a second touchdown in the game with the Broncos, but it wasn't enough to snap what was now a seven-game Raiders losing streak. Desperate to turn around the team, Coach Flores decided to make Bo the feature back in the offense and relegate Marcus Allen to blocking duty. For Bo, the timing of the move couldn't have been more perfect. Not only would the Raiders be playing Seattle on his twenty-fifth birthday, but the contest would be televised to a national Monday-night audience. Now Bo had a chance to prove to the entire nation that he was still a great football player.

And what a show Bo put on for TV viewers and the 60,000-plus fans who packed the Seattle Kingdome that night. First they saw him catch a 14-yard touchdown pass. Then they saw him run for 42 yards to the Seattle 23-yard line. Then they saw him humble one of the most over-hyped players ever to enter the NFL. Brian Bosworth, the 275-pound, rock-solid linebacker from Oklahoma, was considered among the best prospects to join the league in years. Not only that, he was flamboyant, outspoken, and tough, a player one didn't want messing with one's body on a football field.

After Bo's 42-yarder, the Raiders drove down to the 2-yard line. On the next play, Bo took a handoff and ran behind the left tackle toward the sideline before cutting toward the end zone. The only thing between Jackson and the goal line was the intimidating figure of "The Boz." But "The Bo" wasn't easily intimidated. Jackson dipped his head and, like a human battering ram, he plowed into Bosworth. People watching on television could almost hear the entire stadium cry "Oooh!" as the players made contact. The linebacker jerked backward into the end zone as Bo pranced in for the touchdown that gave Los Angeles a 21-7 lead.

But Bo wasn't quite through celebrating his birthday. A few minutes after he had barreled over Bosworth, he threw the entire Kingdome audience for a loop. The Raiders had the ball on their own nine-yard line, when quarterback Marc Wilson pitched out to Bo for another sweep to the left. In an instant, Bo bolted down the sideline, leaving a slew of Seahawks in his wake. Ninety-one yards later, Bo Jackson had scored the longest touchdown from scrimmage in Raiders history, and the eighth-longest run in NFL history. By the end of the 37-14 Los Angeles victory, Bo had scampered for 221 yards, the most ever in a game by a Raiders running back, and the nineteenth highest total in league annals. "Tonight," said ABC "Monday Night Football" analyst Frank Gifford, "Bo Jackson was awesome, simply awesome."

After the game, one Raiders player marveled at how quickly Jackson had pulled away from the Seahawks's swift safety, Ken Easley, on the 91-yard TD run. "Bo made Kenny look like he was running in syrup." Among the many instant Jackson fans created that night was Raiders All-Pro defensive end Howie Long. "I got chills down my spine watching Bo on that run," Long admitted. "The guys on the Seahawks sideline said that when he went by them it felt like the wind created by a speeding car blowing past your face. "Everyone I talk to says the same thing— he's the best runner they have ever seen."

And thousands must have echoed the sentiments of one NFL head coach who said, "Just suppose what he would do if he had the chance to practice this summer like the rest of the running backs."

After gaining 137 total yards the next week against the

Buffalo Bills (78 running), Bo was on a roll as the Raiders went into Kansas City for week 13 of what was a shortened 15-game schedule. It would be Bo's first football game in his baseball hometown and he desperately wanted to excel in front of the fans who had booed him over the summer. It was a great story angle and, naturally, Bo was besieged for media interviews. But instead of ducking the questions, he opened up a bit. The Kansas City game was a perfect forum for him to talk to his critics and a perfect opportunity to get some things off his chest.

"You know," he told reporters, "I get a kick out of hearing people say 'I knew that he could play in the NFL.' Those are the same people who said that I would never make it in the NFL. I get as much fun out of making people liars as I get by playing.

"Sure, the pounding I take in football will eventually take its toll," he continued. "When the time comes to give up a sport, I will. And it will probably be football. But right now football is number one in my heart. Next summer, baseball will be number one in my heart. But I feel I have the ability to display talents in both sports and I'm going to do that. Baseball's what I will make a career out of. But when will I give up football? I don't know. Right now, I'm just taking one day at a time. You can only be young once, and I'm going to have all the fun I can."

Jackson was given even more incentive to have fun at Kansas City's expense when he found that five of ten TV viewers polled by a local station said they would boo Bo before the game. And when he finally ran onto the Arrowhead stadium field, Bo saw a sign with his name painted on the head of a jackass. Bo could only laugh at the idea that the fans thought of him as "Jackson the Jackass."

Unfortunately, Bo never got a chance to silence the hometown hecklers. On his third carry of the game, he sprained his ankle and Tom Flores sat him out for not only the rest of the Kansas City game, but for the last two Raiders contests. The Raiders had too much invested in Bo to turn a minor injury into a career-threatening one. And the Kansas City Royals fans, despite their boos, must have been thankful for the good judgment of the Raiders.

Had Jackson played in all the Raiders games instead of just seven, he probably would have run for twice his '87 season total of 554 yards and still not have shaved an inch off his league-leading total of 6.8 yards per carry. And though Bo started just five games, he was still named to All-Rookie teams by United Press International, *Pro Football Weekly*, and *Football Digest*. Despite Jackson's major contribution, the Raiders still finished the season at a dismal 5–10. "Can we start the whole season over again, right now," Tom Flores said, laughing, "but this time with Bo?"

The Raiders didn't start the 1988 season with Bo or with Tom Flores. Al Davis hired former Denver Broncos assistant coach Mike Shanahan to get the team back on track, but by the time Bo arrived for week seven, the Raiders were already 2–4. If Jackson were to make an immediate impact, it would have to be against the Chiefs. Only this time the Kansas City faithful were more hospitable to Bo since he was coming off his first solid season for the Royals. But although a 25-home run, 68-RBI season had softened the fans' hard-line attitude toward Bo's football career, he was still a member of the archrival Raiders, which meant he was the enemy.

In the days leading up to the Chiefs game, there was some question as to whether Bo would even play. Mike Shanahan had intimated he wouldn't start Jackson, believing it impossible for a player to drop in, six games into the season, learn the new offense Shanahan had installed, and play after only five days of study. Shanahan kept his word. Bo didn't start. He got into the game on the Raiders's second play from scrimmage. When the game ended with Bo rushing for a game-high 70 yards in 21 attempts and 1 touchdown in a 27–17 Raiders victory, Shanahan was singing a different tune.

"Bo surprised me," the coach admitted. "He came to camp in excellent shape and practiced three or four times a day. He adjusted to the offense very quickly and looked like he got stronger as the game went on. He runs like a wide receiver packing fifty extra pounds. I was pleased with the way he handled himself."

"Bo is so fast, it's unbelievable," one Raider offensive lineman said after the game.

Added another, "He really does give us an extra dimension to go with Marcus Allen. When I came off the ball on my block, he was just about there by the time I got to my guy."

After his one-yard touchdown run in the fourth quarter, Bo had hurled the ball as far as he could into the seats filled with Kansas City fans. Had the fans and their reaction to him been on his mind? "The Chiefs defense was on my mind," he said in the locker room. "But as far as the crowd goes, they were wonderful. It was a whole lot better than last year. I only saw one baseball thrown at me."

Jackson started the next nine Raiders games, and, although he didn't have any spectacular games like the one in '87 against Seattle, he produced a solid season. He rushed for 580 yards on 136 carries (for a 4.3 average) and 3 touchdowns. Bo's best game was an 85-yard effort against the eventual Super Bowl champion San Francisco 49ers, and his longest touchdown run was a 22-yarder against the Chiefs. Those two performances sparked a three-game

Raider winning streak, but four losses in their last five games kept Los Angeles out of the playoffs, with a 7–9 record. For Bo, playing two sports was one thing; single-handedly reviving the Raiders was quite another.

When Bo joined the Raiders for game six of the 1989 season, he was coming off his most glorious season as a baseball player—32 home runs, 105 RBI's, All-Star Game MVP—but a playoff spot for Los Angeles already looked like a long shot at best. The team was in a mini-turmoil after losing three straight following an opening-game victory. And so Al Davis, the ultimate power behind the "Pride and Poise" boys, abruptly fired Mike Shanahan and hired former Raiders offensive lineman Art Shell as the first black head coach in NFL history. The headline-making move may have upstaged Bo's return, but it paid off immediately, as in their last Bo-less game, the Raiders beat the lowly New York Jets, 14–7, in a nationally tele-vised Monday-nighter.

With a new head coach at the helm and Jackson back in silver and black for the October 15 game against the Kan-sas City Chiefs, football pundits speculated about the focus of the offensive game plan of the Raiders. *Sports Illustrated* said the Raiders offense had been "schizophrenic" since Jackson joined the team in 1987. With Bo in the backfield, the magazine claimed, the Raiders had been more run-oriented, even though that strategy had had little bearing on the team's record. But as offensive backfield coach Joe Scannella pointed out, Shell liked the power-running game used by Tom Flores, as opposed to the "deceptive kinds of runs" favored by Shanahan. "It will be interesting to see," the magazine mused, "if Shell's offense, which seems to fit Jackson perfectly, will be more productive as well as more ground-oriented than that of his two predecessors."

Those questions were answered almost immediately as

Jackson gained 85 yards on 11 carries and scored a touchdown in a 20–14 victory over the Chiefs. Bo was the workhorse in a 10–7 loss the following week against the Philadelphia Eagles. Though he carried the ball 20 times, the tough Eagles defense held Jackson to just 79 yards. But Bo was just warming up. The first two games seemed like his personal training season, considering what he did to the Washington Redskins in week eight. With the Raiders holding a 17–10 lead early in the third quarter, Bo busted through the Skins defense for a 73-yard touchdown run. Then he delighted Raiders fans with 71 yards in his 18 other carries and, after the 37–24 victory, served notice that the Raiders, now 4–4, were back. "This win just makes it tougher for whoever we play next week."

Unfortunately for the Cincinnati Bengals, they were next on the Raiders schedule. Bo wasted little time turning the Bengals defense into a bunch of pussycats, producing a seven-yard touchdown run just three and a half minutes into the game. About nine minutes later, Bo made NFL history. He took a handoff from quarterback Jay Schroeder at the Raiders 8-yard line, swept to the left sideline, and then, like a blur, broke downfield for a 92-yard touchdown romp. Not only was the TD dash a Raiders record, but it was the first time in NFL history that a player had scored 2 touchdown runs of 90 or more yards. Jackson ended up with 159 yards in a 28–7 Los Angeles victory.

"Bo is as advertised," Bengals coach Sam Wyche said after the game. "He is one of those rare ones that comes along only so often. I hope everyone enjoys watching him now because he will go down as one of the legends of the game."

Bo wasn't as impressed with himself. "Just another day at the office," he said. "The people responsible for my runs are really the linemen and my fullback. I just do what I can do. I don't try to do things I know I can't do."

Jackson couldn't keep the Raiders rolling against San Diego the following week, as they lost to the Chargers, 14–12, despite Bo's 103-yard effort. But in week 11, against the Houston Oilers, both Bo and the Raiders were stymied. With Art Shell's team down, 20–7, late in the third quarter, Jackson, who had gained 54 yards on 11 carries to that point, took himself out of the game, saying he was "a little tired." After the game, he claimed that he had felt "a twinge" in the top of his left quadricep muscle and came out for fear of pulling a hamstring, an injury that could sideline him for weeks. The quadricep injury had severely hampered his base-stealing during the second half of the baseball season, when he said he played at only "seventy-five percent."

But as they did during similar situations while Bo was at Auburn, the media began wondering about Bo's "toughness," and his ability to handle adversity. The Oilers, whose aggressive defense had tamed Jackson, had no such questions about Bo's tenacity. His first run of the game was for 14 yards and might have been a 91-yard touchdown run had not Houston free safety Jeff Donaldson struggled to bring Bo down. "Man, he's a load," Donaldson said. "He's a freight train. It's real scary when he's one arm-tackle away from breaking a ninety-yarder."

"I've never seen anything like the way the guy can outrun defensive backs," chimed in an Oilers defender.

"When Bo ran the first time," Oilers defensive end Sean Jones observed, 'I counted fifty-nine thousand people standing up. I've never seen a guy like this. Every time he touches the ball, the fans gasp. He's incredible and he runs with authority. Anybody who says Bo is not tough is wrong."

In 6 games, including the Houston loss, Jackson had gained 624 yards in 95 carries, for an NFL-leading 6.6-yard average, and scored 4 touchdowns, already his best totals in his three abbreviated Raider seasons. At this rate, Bo was on target for a 1,000-yard rushing season, considered the magical mark for running backs. It was official: Bo was now an established NFL star and he was receiving the accolades to support his status. Art Shell even went so far as to compare Jackson to two of the greatest running backs ever.

"The guy has the qualities of Jim Brown," Shell insisted. "He's got that kind of explosiveness, that kind of speed. And when he turns the doggone corner, he's got the speed and quickness of an O. J. Simpson. If Bo continues to play the way he's playing, I'm sure he is a future Hall of Fame player." Everybody knew Bo was strong.

Everybody knew Bo was fast. But what went on inside Bo's head before he took off with a football?

"Right before the snap," he told ESPN, the 24-hour sports cable network, "I'm looking the linebacker right in the eye. I don't want him to know, I don't want him to think, 'This guy's timid and he is afraid.' I look him in the eye because I know wherever I go, he is going. You have to be the attacker instead of the attackee. Every time I touch the ball, every time I block, I try to attack the opponent. I try to catch them off guard or beat them to the punch. Upon getting the ball, I wait for my blocks. I stop breathing, everything gets quiet, and when the hole's there, I hit it. Then everything comes back to life. I hear the people cheering, I hear the blocking going on, but that's all behind me at that point. The only thing I'm trying to do is get to the goal line."

Going into the '89 season finale against the New York Giants, Bo had amassed 915 yards rushing, which included a 114-yard effort in week 14 against the Phoenix Cardinals. For Bo to bag a 1,000-yard season (over just 11 games), and give the Raiders a glimmer of hope for the play-offs, he would have to gain 85 yards against the NFL's fourth-best run defense. Gerald Riggs of the Washington Redskins had been the only back all season to gain more than 100 yards against the Giants, but the playoff-bound team, known in New York as the "Big Blue," had never contended with the Big Bo.

"He's probably one of the most complete backs I've seen on film this year," Giants linebacker Gary Reasons said a couple of days before the game. "Rarely do you get a guy who runs well inside or outside with power."

"He's a guy you've got to string out," observed New York nose guard Erik Howard, "get support from the out-side. Don't give him any seams and take the holes away from him. Most of the guys we faced like to cut it back. But Bo's the kind of guy who tries to get the outside, and if it's there, he'll take it. He's got great speed, and if he gets into the open field, he'll be a hard guy to catch."

Giants All-Pro linebacker Carl Banks was also impressed with Bo's highlight films, but wanted a bit more proof before anointing Jackson as the NFL's top runner. "We've faced backs with good speed before," Banks said. "I know the guy can run just by looking at him. He's dangerous inside and out. But I can't tell you he's the best back we've ever seen. I'll let you know after the game."

The Giants went into the game fired up. Not only were they playing in front of their home fans on a cold, windy day in the New Jersey Meadowlands, but they knew that a victory would give them the NFL East Division cham-pionship. When the tough defense by the Giants stopped Bo for no gain the first four times he had the ball, few doubted the outcome. New York held Bo to a measly 35 yards on 10 carries and dominated the Raiders, 34–17.

Bo Jackson didn't need to dwell on the disappointment of not making the playoffs or falling short of the 1,000-yard plateau. The man had produced one of the most amazing years in the history of professional sports. He had proven to America that he still knew football. He could now look forward to a well-deserved two-month vacation, a time when he could hunt and fish and spend time with his family. After all, he could go for a 1,000-yard season in 1990. Then again, Bo was probably hoping he wouldn't play in enough games to get the chance. Playing fewer football games would mean he was playing more baseball games—in October. And what self-respecting two-sport athlete wouldn't trade a 1,000-yard season for a World Series ring?

Bo
Knows
Baseball—Finally

During the winter of 1988, Bo Jackson had little time to revel in the success he had achieved in the first year of playing his "hobby" sport—football. He was too busy thinking about how his 1987 baseball season had deteriorated, about how he had been benched and booed, and about what he would have to do on the field to win over the Royals management, teammates, and fans.

Still, the experience of the 1987 baseball season had caused Bo such anguish that he wouldn't publicly commit himself to the Royals for 1988. The conventional wisdom, however, was that Bo would be back, especially since he would forfeit more than $500,000 in base salary and bonuses if he quit the game. Bo's decision became apparent when he went to Auburn in January to work out with the baseball team. Then he showed up at the Royals's Fort Myers spring training camp a week earlier than his teammates. The sprained ankle Jackson had suffered at the end of the football season had healed and he seemed more determined than ever to prove his worth as a ballplayer.

But while Bo worked on refining his batting stroke by spending hours in the cage, Kansas City management was telling people that their honeymoon with Bo was over. If Bo didn't produce—and soon—it would be *"bang, zoom"* to the minors. No longer would the Royals let Bo dictate his future with the team. No longer would other players be shuffled around to get Bo in the lineup. No longer would a job be handed to him on a silver platter. If Bo Jackson wanted to be a starting outfielder in Kansas City, he would have to earn the position, especially since the team was high on Gary Thurman, who had replaced Bo in left field the previous September.

"I see a tremendously competitive situation liable to develop in left field between Bo and Gary," Royals general manager John Schuerholz announced before camp opened. "And if Bo is not the opening-day left fielder, we'd probably send him to the minors. If we didn't, we'd be accomplices in not allowing Bo to develop his skills. That would not be good for the development of his baseball career.

"But if Bo decides he wants to dedicate himself to baseball," Schuerholz continued, "I'm convinced he'll be an outstanding player for a long, long time and provide many years of baseball excitement to this community."

Bo did dedicate himself that spring, just as he did during the 1987 training camp. He was beginning to realize that in a sport like baseball, in which skills had to be constantly honed and refined, his natural ability would take him only so far. He even said he would go to the minors if the Royals thought that was where he belonged. But Bo wanted no part of Triple-A ball this year, and to ensure that he went north with the Royals, he again took hours of batting practice, shagged hundreds of fly balls, and got off to a hot start during the exhibition season. If Bo didn't stick with the team now, Jackson's agent Richard Woods offered, it would be because the Royals wanted "to get back at him" for playing football.

That vindictive the Royals were not. Besides, how could they farm out a guy who hit .298 in 57 spring at-bats, with a team-leading 5 homers and 12 runs batted in? As his team was ready to break camp, manager John Wathan announced that Bo would be the starting left fielder for the Royals on opening day. Gary Thurman? He had batted just .185 and was relegated to the bench.

But after the first few weeks of the season, it appeared that Jackson and Thurman would soon be swapping positions. Bo's big bugaboo, the strikeout, was back. In his first 100 at-bats of 1988, Jackson fanned 33 times, an average more than twice as high as his batting average, which stood at a dismal .115. Bo refused to let the slow start get him down. "I've learned," he said, "that the harder you try in this game, the more you press and then the more you mess up."

Jackson kept coming to the park early for extra batting practice and his hard work soon paid off. In May he got into one of the best hitting grooves of his young career. During the month he hit safely in 21 of 27 games, batted .330, hit 5 home runs, drove in 19 runs, and stole 9 bases, statistics that earned him accolades as his team's Player of the Month. But Bo's barrage was abruptly halted on the last day of the month when he tore his left hamstring running out a ground ball at Cleveland. At that point he was hitting .309 with 9 home runs, and John Schuerholz thought Bo had become the best player on the Royals. "Let's face it," the GM said, "Bo's improved dramatically."

It was while Bo was sidelined for 29 games in June that his Royals teammates, like Schuerholz, started to appreciate his ability and his turnaround. Second baseman Frank White revealed that "there have been a lot of times when guys get to second base and tell me that they think Bo is the most improved player in the game. I've got to say that I agree."

Willie Wilson, who had been one of the loudest critics of Jackson's decision to play football, was now one of Bo's biggest boosters. "We blamed him for all our problems last season when we lost the pennant," Wilson admitted. "But at a time when he needed us the most, we abandoned him. He didn't need that abuse, especially from his teammates." The center fielder also noticed how much Jackson had improved defensively in the outfield. At the time of his injury, Bo had thrown out nine runners on the bases. "In '87, Bo was making aggressive mistakes," Wilson observed. "Now he takes his time, knows the speed of the runner, and knows what to do with the ball. He's a fast learner."

Added Royals pitcher Mark Gubicza: "To me, Bo's one of the best left fielders in the game now. His quickness and his arm are a tough combo to beat."

First baseman George Brett had become something of a mentor to Bo, and when Jackson returned to the lineup in July, the Royals' long-time superstar led the cheers. "Just call me the president and charter member of the Bo Jackson Fan Club," Brett said. "Nobody has awed me like that man. Nobody has impressed me as much. He's the greatest athlete I've ever seen."

Even opposing players were jumping on Bo's baseball bandwagon. "Bo can hit home runs to beat you and he can steal bases to beat you," raved Paul Molitor of the Milwaukee Brewers. "He can beat you with his arm or with his glove. He can do so many things to beat you that it's frightening."

No better was the talent of multifaceted Mr. Jackson displayed than at Boston's fabled Fenway Park on the afternoon of Saturday, July 16. Bo stepped to the plate in the second inning against flaky Red Sox right-hander Oil Can Boyd. When Bo connected with a Boyd slider, the ball soared toward the 50-foot center-field wall, which is about 450 feet from home plate. The ball hit about 45 feet up the wall, 8 feet higher than the top of the fabled "Green Monster" in left field. Some people who saw the blast said the ball was still in ascent when it hit the wall and that it was probably one of the longest home runs ever hit at Fenway. The ever-quotable Boyd offered his estimate to be about 800 feet.

Three innings after this display of his raw power, Bo gave the 35,000 fans at Fenway a glimpse of his speed, agility, outfield range, and arm all in one play. With a Boston runner at second, Red Sox catcher Rich Gedman launched a drive to left center field that seemed destined to be an extra-base hit in the gap. Jackson, running full speed, leaped toward center field and, with his body parallel to the ground and his glove outstretched, caught the ball. He landed hard on the turf, rolled out of the fall, sprang up, and threw a fast-ball strike to second, which stopped the runner from tagging up and going to third. The partisan Red Sox fans gave Jackson a standing ovation after the play, after it was replayed on the scoreboard, and when he ran in after the inning.

"It was a great play," Rich Gedman said, by way of an understatement. "One of the best I've ever seen."

Added Red Sox manager Joe Morgan: "I've never seen anything like it in thirty-seven years of professional baseball."

But for Bo in the second half of the '88 season, days like the one in Fenway were few and far between. In the 46 games before his hamstring injury, Jackson batted .309 with 9 homers, 30 RBI's, and 14 stolen bases. In the 46 games after the layoff, he batted .192 with 11 homers, 24 ribbies, and 8 steals.

"If he hadn't gotten hurt and missed those five weeks," George Brett said, "his stats would be pretty awesome right now. When he came back it took him two and a half to three weeks before he started hitting."

"I'm not hitting the way I can," Bo admitted in late August, "but I'm hitting the long ball every now and then, and that's keeping my spirits up. But I don't worry about my average. I'm not a person to worry about stats. I just want to go out and play good baseball."

Sports Illustrated theorized that Bo's second-half falloff—his second in two years—had to do with the opening of football training camps. Since Jackson's cumulative second-half average was .203, the magazine wondered if, like young boys whose school marks drop when baseball season begins, Bo's mind was turning to football while the Royals were trying to win pennants. Was Bo thinking more about a playbook than the third base coach's signs?

"That's absolutely absurd," GM Schuerholz said about the *S.I.* article. "I think it's an unfair criticism of Bo to say his mind has wandered. His mind hasn't wandered—he tore up a hamstring, that's all."

Could the slump be attributed to the fatigue created by almost nonstop professional competition? Was the long, hot baseball season just too much for Bo?

"I don't know about that," John Wathan said. "But coping with the grind of six months and one hundred sixty-two games—as opposed to playing a football game every seven days—is something he had to learn for himself. We all think about what he could do if it weren't for the football thing. For instance, he could be a great switch-hitter if he could work on it during the winter, but . . ."

Even with the injury, the second-half slump, and the

team-leading 146 strikeouts, Bo became the Royals's first "25-25 player," with 25 home runs and 27 stolen bases. He also drove in 68 runs, scored 63, and batted .318 at home, which sparked a renewed affection between Bo and Royals rooters. "Everything's worked out well," John Schuerholz admitted. "It's like all is forgiven, all is forgotten. The fans in this community have accepted Bo for the gifted athlete that he is."

If Bo was pleased about being back in the good graces of Kansas City fans, he wasn't letting on. After all, his three-year, $1.06 million contract was up. "Sure I'm happy about it," he admitted, "but I don't go out there to please the public. I'm just trying to do my job as best I can. It's not up to me to say whether I've played well."

Bo certainly played well enough to soften the hard-line stance the organization had taken with him before the season began. This off-season there would be no inflammatory quotes, no ultimatums about ending his football career. The Royals front office would just quietly bite its lip and pray Bo didn't get some knee joints rearranged by an overaggressive middle linebacker.

"Bo knows how we feel about the football career and we know how he feels," John Schuerholz told the *Kansas City Star.* "My perspective is a little selfish, of course, because it's only from a baseball standpoint. Bo's perspective is through his own eyes, with his own objectives, and with his own desire.

"I think that while he's a good ballplayer now, and he's contributed to our team, he could be a better ballplayer and contribute even more if he were not playing another professional sport. From my selfish standpoint, I'd like to fantasize how much better he could be if he would give himself entirely to baseball."

But as Bo Jackson would show Schuerholz, the Royals, and the entire baseball world in 1989, he *could* play another professional sport and still make some people's fantasies a reality.

10

Bo Knows Superstardom

Once the 1988 football season had ended, the first order of business for Bo Jackson's agent, Richard Woods (who had become Bo's sole representative), was to negotiate a new contract with the Royals. Woods was in a great bargaining position. His client had come out of the football wars unscathed and had produced 1988 baseball numbers that, if projected out over a full season, would have ranked him with the game's very top players. The Royals also knew that Jackson didn't need baseball to earn a living. But with Bo ineligible for contract arbitration until 1990 and the Royals owning his rights until after the 1992 season, Woods wasn't about to be confrontational. "There's absolutely no question Bo loves Kansas City, the Royals organization, and baseball," Woods said. "He definitely plans to be back in Kansas City."

Negotiations with the Royals went smoothly, and by the start of spring training Bo had signed a one-year contract for $585,000. Although the one-year deal would make Jackson eligible for arbitration the following season (a major advantage should he produce stratospheric statistics), some people wondered why Bo didn't use his success in football as a tool to get more money from Kansas City. Of course, these were the same people who labeled him "greedy" when he signed with the Raiders in 1987.

"Most people have got the wrong impression about Bo Jackson where there's money concerned," Bo told *Kansas City Star* writer Bob Nightengale after the signing. "I can live with the money. I can live without it. I'm not in this game to get all the money that I can and say the heck with this sport. Or to say: 'Hey, either you give me this, or I'm going to do this.' Or: 'You give me this, or I'm going to do that.' That's not me.

"When the time comes for me to make big money, if it's time, I'll make it. I'm in no rush. The money's not going no place. I'm not going no place. It's just like this two-sport thing. This is just the way I want to spend my time. It has nothing to do with being Jim Thorpe, or trying to be the world's greatest athlete. It's just me."

Once spring training began, Bo wasted little time authoring another one of those patented folk tales. On a sunny Florida afternoon in early March, the kind baseball writers get all gushy about, the Royals were playing against the Red Sox at their Baseball City complex. Jackson came to bat in the second inning against Oil Can Boyd. That's right, the same Oil Can Boyd against whom Bo launched a mammoth blast the previous year at Fenway Park. Boyd's first pitch was a mediocre fast ball that made a hitter's eyes bug out. Bo almost jumped out of his Nikes on the swing and smacked the ball over the 71-foot-high center-field fence, approximately 400 feet from home plate. The ball didn't stop traveling until it bounced up against the inside of a wire fence 40 yards beyond the outfield barrier. This latest Bo blast was estimated at 515 feet.

"It was utter disbelief," Royals manager John Wathan said, "that a human being could hit a ball that far."

At the beginning of the new season, however, Bo was as cold as the early April weather. During the first week and a half Jackson batted just .167 with 2 home runs and 4 RBI's. Despite the slow start, he was showing subtle signs of improvement in every aspect of his game. Take his approach to hitting. In the fifth game of the season, the Royals were trailing the Red Sox, 1–0, in the top of the seventh inning. With Roger Clemens on the mound for Boston, things looked pretty secure to the Fenway faithful. "I'm going to get him," Jackson told his teammates, even though Clemens had struck out Bo 9 of 13 times in his career. True to his word, Jackson connected with a 90-plus m.p.h. Clemens fast ball and smacked a line drive that just cleared the fence in right center field.

"He'd never shown that he could hit that pitch," Clemens said after the Royals won, 2–1, in ten innings. "I had a lot on that ball, but I tip my hat to him. He whistled his bat through the strike zone like nothing I'd ever seen, and he hit the ball so hard I couldn't even turn around to see it go over the fence."

There were also positive changes in Bo's base running and outfield play. When he first joined the Royals, he simply relied on his great speed when running the bases. But after watching the way the pros shortened distances by turning at the bag, he began to cut the bases as well as any player. His lack of experience on fly balls caused him to run at odd angles in the outfield. But during the '89 season he began making over-the-head catches he never would have made in previous years.

"Bo never has to be told anything twice," said a Royals coach. "He'll just study something and figure it out."

Still, there were a lot of so-called "experts" Bo could not please; the ones more interested in statistics than subtleties. Just two poor weeks early in the season and those questions were starting to be asked again. Did football take too much out of him? Would he always be a schizophrenic baseball player? Would he ever realize his "potential"?

Bo began answering the questions on April 15 in Toronto. With the Royals trailing 5–0, in the second inning, he hit a towering two-run homer into the left-field seats at Exhibition Stadium. Later he would get two more hits and an RBI to spark a 10–5 come-from-behind victory.

For Jackson, that game was like shooting out of the blocks after hearing the starting gun go off. Over the next week he was an offensive machine, hitting .348 with 3 homers, 7 RBI's, 6 runs scored, and 5 stolen bases. The performance earned him American League Player of the Week honors for the first time in his career and more praise from players and scouts.

"He doesn't even look like the same ballplayer anymore," observed New York Yankees scout Mike Ferraro. "His progress is amazing. To see the way he is now, and the way he was when he first came up, is just incredible to me."

"I don't know how long he's going to be able to play both sports, but he's improved his ballplaying," said Red Sox pitcher Wes Gardner, who gave up a Jackson home run during a three-game Royals sweep of Boston at Fenway. "At the plate, he's more patient. He's not trying to pull everything like he was last year. He's found out he has power the other way, and that he doesn't have to pull everything to hit it a mile. He hits a lot like [Jose] Canseco does."

It wasn't surprising to hear Jackson's name mentioned in the same sentence with the American League's 1988 Most Valuable Player. What was surprising was that the talk would start before the second month of the season. The baseball pundits began speculating about whether Bo could become the second player in two years—and in history, for that matter—to join the 40-homer, 40-steals club. Canseco had done it the previous season with 42 round-trippers and 40 stolen bases. Jackson, with six homers and eight steals by April 24, was already ahead of Canseco's 1988 pace.

"To tell you the truth," John Wathan said, "I think he has the potential to be a fifty–fifty man once he learns the strike zone better and swings at only good pitches."

"I can't worry about things like 'forty-forty clubs,' " Bo insisted. "Sure it would be nice, but you know, I'd just rather not think about it. I'd rather not talk about it. When you start doing that, you put too much pressure on yourself and you put ideas in people's minds, and they run away with it. I'm not a statistician. I just want to go out and play. If it [40–40] happens, it happens. If not, I'm sure not going to lose any sleep over it."

It was probably inevitable that Bo's baseball breakout would bring with it the seemingly endless debate about his two-sport career. For example, Ron Rapoport, a sports-writer for the *Los Angeles Daily News*, suggested that football was more "a fallback" than "a hobby" for Jackson, and that with Bo's emergence as a baseball star, it was probably time to bid the Raiders farewell. Rapoport wrote that Bo "has not exactly delivered the goods the way the Raiders had hoped."

Rapoport noted that Jackson appeared to enjoy his baseball career more and more, that he liked being a star in Kansas City, that he liked the freedom and privacy the long baseball season offered. If the Royals dangled a big-money, multi-year deal in front of him, Rapoport wondered, one that asked him to stop risking his body on a football field, could Bo possibly say no?

Washington Post columnist Tony Kornheiser suggested

that the question shouldn't even be asked. "If this is the year Bo Jackson becomes Mickey Mantle," Kornheiser wrote, "everyone will want to know when Bo will forget about this cockamamie football-baseball thing. Speaking for the minority, I hope he continues the romance. It should be clear he loves playing both sports. Why make him choose? To satisfy someone else's sense of neatness? People ought to applaud his commitment to the joy of sports, shout hurrah for the year-round pleasure he gives. Let the guy have his fun. It's his life, isn't it?

"Bo Jackson's sensational in April for the Royals and tremendous in November for the Raiders. Considering his athletic ability, Jackson ought to play more sports. Don't let him get stale. Spread him around. Start a Bo Jackson's Sport-of-the-Month club. If this is May, it must be horse racing. Can Easy Goer carry two hundred twenty-five pounds?"

After Jackson had single-handedly destroyed the Red Sox in late April, Boston manager Joe Morgan said that "the way he's hitting now, I'm glad we won't see him again for a few months. I'll just catch him on the highlight films each night." Indeed, some of Jackson's performances were so spectacular that television stations would have been justified playing them each day on the nightly news. Bo Jackson, the man Baltimore Orioles scout Ed Farmer told *Sports Illustrated* (which featured Jackson on a June cover headlined "Nobody Hits 'Em like Bo") had become "the best player in the game today," had also become a human highlight film. Let's go to the videotape.

In the sixth inning of a May 16 game against the Minnesota Twins at the Metrodome, Jackson hit a ball that landed in the right-field upper deck. It was the first time in the stadium's history that a right-handed batter ever hit a ball to that part of the Metrodome. "I hit it off the end of the bat," Jackson said later.

At Texas on May 23, Jackson faced one of the toughest pitchers for him to hit—the legendary speedballing hurler Nolan Ryan. Jackson had struck out six successive times over two games against Ryan before this particular at-bat. Ryan had always wondered what would happen if Bo had ever connected on one of his heaters. On this day, he found out. Let's go to the videotape: The first pitch brushed Bo off the plate. On the second pitch, Ryan threw one of his patented 95-mile-per-hour fast balls an inch or two under Bo's chin, knocking him to the dirt. Jackson dusted himself off and glared at Ryan for a few seconds. Two pitches later, Jackson hit another express from Ryan into the center-field bleachers of Arlington's stadium, 461 feet away, the longest ever hit there. "They'd better get a new tape measure," said Bo.

Later on Bo's old high-school baseball coach, Terry Brasseale, asked his former player if Ryan's close shaves had scared him. "He said, 'Hell, yes,' " Brasseale related, "but then Bo said he got sick and tired of Ryan doing that to him. Bo always seems to respond to a challenge."

On June 5 in Seattle's Kingdome, an apt name for a place in which to create a legend, Bo made what is now simply referred to as the "The Throw." Let's go to the videotape: It's the bottom of the tenth inning, score tied 3–3. With two out and speedy Harold Reynolds of the Mariners running with the pitch, left-handed batter Scott Bradley lined a Steve Barr fast ball down the left-field line. With one foot on the warning track, Jackson grabbed the ball and in the same motion threw the ball home, attempting to stop what seemed like a sure winning run. The ball sailed approximately 300 feet on a fly from the track into catcher Bob Boone's waiting glove and Reynolds was out at the plate. The Royals won the game in the thirteenth inning, 5–3.

Let's go to the audiotape:

"I thought the game was over when I rounded second," Reynolds said afterward. "When I saw where the ball was headed, I put it in overdrive, and when I rounded third I was flat-out flying. I saw Darnell Coles [the on-deck hitter] with his arms up, telling me to come in standing. Then, suddenly, he was waving me down. I couldn't believe that, but I went into a courtesy slide. Next thing I know, Boone is tagging me out. I couldn't believe what happened until I saw a replay. I still don't believe it."

"There is no one on the planet who can make that throw," Bob Boone said, "but Bo did. A number of players might have done it with a step to crank up. He did it flat-footed. Unbelievable, just unbelievable."

"I took the ball off the wall, turned, and threw," Bo explained. "It was preplanned. I knew Reynolds would be trying to score. There was no need to hit any cutoff man. The ball went straight, never tailed or sailed. It was just one of those things. I'm not impressed with how far I can hit a ball and all that."

"Bo doesn't make a lot out of what he does on the field," Richard Woods told *The New York Times*. "He never talks to me about anything but maybe throwing a guy out. He likes that. It fires him up. That's better than a touchdown run. He knows he can do that, but he was criticized for his defense. Assists are something he's proud of."

Bo's critics may have regarded his skills as merely mortal, but baseball fans had become absolutely entranced with his otherworldly feats on the field of dreams. When the All-Star teams were announced at the end of June, Jackson had received the most votes of any American League player. Almost 2,000,000 fans (1,748,696 to be exact) punched Bo Jackson's name on the All-Star ballot, a clear message to the baseball establishment that Jackson was now a bona fide superstar. Jackson's reaction to the honor? Typical for him, he seemed unimpressed.

"If I'm chosen, great," Bo told *USA Today*. "If I'm not, that's great, too. I'll just put a new line on my fishing rod, get my trolling motor, and go out fishing with some of my buddies."

As the first half of the season was ending, Bo tuned up for his appearance in the mid-summer classic. He supplied some Fourth of July fireworks with a 2-homer game against the All-Star-laden Oakland Athletics, and became a 20-home-run, 20-stolen-base man for the second straight season. And five days later, he hit his twenty-first homer in the eleventh inning to give the Royals a 4–3 win over Chicago. With Bo leading the way, Kansas City went into the All-Star break with a 49–37 record and only three and a half games behind the defending American League champion Athletics.

One of the most intriguing questions before baseball's star showcase concerned where Bo would hit in the American League's starting lineup. Jackson had been the clean-up hitter for the Royals since May 23 (the day he took Ryan deep in Texas), but with sluggers like Jose Canseco, Mark McGwire, Cal Ripken, Gary Gaetti, and Kirby Puckett at manager Tony La Russa's disposal, Bo couldn't possibly be in the heart of the order, let alone the number-four man. But La Russa knew the perfect spot for such a weapon as Jackson. He not only remembered the two-homer game Bo had against his A's before the break, but thought about a game in mid-June when Jackson beat his club with speed.

"We were up a run in the ninth inning and Bo led off," La Russa recalled in New York's *Newsday*. "He hit a chopper in the hole and beat it easily, got picked off first and beat the throw to second easily, then scored the tying run on a single. He led off again in the eleventh inning, stole second off a left-hander [Rick Honeycutt] with the best pickoff move in the league, and scored the winning run on a single.''

In La Russa's eyes, Bo Jackson was nothing if not a catalyst; a pretty powerful catalyst at that. So, as the National League had done with a speedy slugger like Willie Mays 21 years before, the American League put Bo Jackson in the leadoff spot for the sixtieth All-Star Game in Anaheim.

"I think it will make for a lot of excitement right away," La Russa predicted.

The manager turned out to be prescient, but Bo didn't wait until his first at-bat to create excitement. In the top of the first, he stopped a potential National League rally with a running grab of Pedro Guerrero's line drive, a poke that seem destined for extra bases. When Bo led off the bottom of the inning, he was facing the veteran right-hander Rick Reuschel, who features an assortment of breaking pitches and changes of speed. Reuschel's second pitch to Jackson was what is called "a backup slider." It's a pitch that looks like a fast ball, but from a right-handed pitcher it will tail down inside to a right-handed batter, moving somewhat like a screwball. Bo took a massive but somewhat awkward swing at the pitch, hitting it almost the way one would hit a golf ball. The ball jumped off Bo's bat as if shot out of a cannon, and in what seemed like an instant it sailed over the center-field fence, almost 450 feet from home plate. Jackson had become only the ninth player in All-Star Game history to homer in his first at-bat, and only the fifth to hit a home run while leading off an All-Star Game.

"I'd heard about his power and strength, and I saw it firsthand tonight," Rick Reuschel said after the game.

And Wade Boggs, who followed Bo's blast in the first with a homer of his own, added, "When he hit that ball, I said to myself, 'Oh, my God.' It was a sight to watch."

But the Bo show didn't stop with his prodigious shot. Later in the game he displayed his great speed to beat out an infield grounder and steal a base, then drove in the winning run on an out in the American League's 5–3 victory. La Russa's strategy had worked. Not only did Bo become the only player besides Willie Mays to hit a home run and steal a base in the same All-Star Game, but his complete performance earned him the game's Most Valuable Player award.

"Bo can do anything," said San Diego Padres outfielder and three-time NL batting champion Tony Gwynn when asked for his reaction to Bo's performance. "It's scary. He changes the way people think of the game. He's redefining the game as we speak. I'm a believer."

During the post-game press conference, Jackson was asked what his biggest thrill of the evening had been. Was he impressed with the flight of his majestic home run?

"Nah," he told the media, a smile stretching across his face. "I think I got more of a kick out of watching those F-four jet planes fly over than me hitting the home run. What can I say? Everyone has his weaknesses. F-fours are mine."

After everyone had a good laugh, Bo got a little more serious.

"Doing what Willie Mays did will be something special when I can sit back and tell the story to my grandkids," he said. "But I still hate to compare myself to the great players of the past. They did their thing then. I'm doing mine now. You start thinking you're the next Willie Mays and the next Babe Ruth, and you can get caught up in that. That kind of thing can get you out of the game quicker than you can wink an eye.''

The evening of the All-Star Game was Bo Jackson's night in more way than one. Jackson hadn't just been all over the field, he'd been all over the tube. When millions of television viewers weren't watching Bo's dazzling array of baseball skills during the game, they saw Bo playing a wide variety of sports in a Nike athletic-shoe commercial. The ''Bo Knows'' ad spot premiered that night and was immediately declared an artistic success.

The 60-second ad showed Jackson in action in a sport, immediately followed by the comment of a star performer in that sport. Jackson hits a baseball and then Los Angeles Dodgers outfielder Kirk Gibson says, ''Bo knows baseball.''

Jackson eludes some tacklers and Los Angeles Rams quarterback Jim Everett says, ''Bo knows football.'' Then basketball star Michael Jordan, runner Joan Benoit Samuelson, a women's pro-cycling team, and a group of bodybuilders attest to Jackson's prowess in their sports. (Scenes of Bo playing cricket and soccer landed on the cutting room floor.)

The commercial takes a comic turn when tennis star John McEnroe asks incredulously, ''Bo knows tennis?''

Then, after a clip of Jackson playing hockey, superstar Wayne Gretzky just looks into the camera and says simply, ''No,'' in an amazed tone of voice.

The commercial ends with Jackson trying to play a guitar onstage with another famous Bo—musician Bo Diddley, who composed and performed the music in the ad. As Jackson struggles to make some rock guitar riffs, Diddley points a finger at him and snaps, ''Bo, you don't know Diddley.'' The clever, award-winning commercial was so well received by the public that Bo and his agent probably wished they were getting a cut of each sneaker sale. Nike, of course, was more than pleased that Jackson had a spectacular All-Star Game the same night the spot debuted. Bo knows timing.

"My feet haven't touch the ground," said Scott Bedbury, Nike's ad director. "Now it's on to the Super Bowl."

Nike had signed Bo to a six-figure endorsement contract in 1986 after he joined the Royals, and the first television spot, an award-winner called "Cross-Training by Bo Jackson," appeared in 1988 after he'd joined the Raiders. The ad showed Bo bicycling, long-distance running, and stuffing a basketball, and ended with Jackson saying a line intended to jab at his critics: "Another day, another hobby."

A print campaign in 1988, which pictured Bo wearing shoulder pads and carrying a bat, read: "If Bo Jackson takes up any more hobbies, we're ready." (Early in 1990, the same ad became a 60-foot-high mural painted on the side of a building at Hollywood and Vine in Los Angeles.)

And a 1989 print ad called "The Jackson 5" showed Bo in different poses—with a basketball, a tennis racket, a bicycle, a barbell, and running.

"The key to the Nike spots," said Bo's agent, Richard Woods, "is that Bo pokes a little fun at himself."

If there is an irony in Nike's celebration of Jackson's versatility, it's that the company was originally upset that Bo had chosen baseball over football back in 1986. The trade journal *Advertising Age* had reported that year that Bo's deal with Nike would pay him much more money if he played football (a claim Bo's agents at the time denied). Whether such a deal existed or not, Nike had to feel that Jackson would be more valuable to the company as a pro-football player than as a minor-leaguer in baseball. But the clever commercials Nike generated after Bo became a two-sport pro athlete made "cross-trainers" the company's fastest-growing shoe line.

Bo seemed to be having as much fun making the spots as Nike was counting its profits from them. One of the outakes of the "Bo Knows" ad showed Jackson covering up the first three letters of his rectangular "Turbo" electric guitar and saying into the camera, "This is my own personal guitar. See, 'Bo.' "

Another showed Bo doing some down-and-dirty riffing with the Diddley band, compelling the musical Bo to tell Jackson, "Bo, you do know Diddley."

Surprisingly, Woods wasn't much interested in parlaying Bo's sudden fame into more endorsement deals like the one with Nike. Not that there weren't plenty of offers. Every kind of promoter and hustler contacted Woods, but the agent wasn't about to take just any diddley deal that proposed to use Bo Jackson's name and image to sell a product. "We've had dozens of offers to endorse this and appear here and there, do this or that," Woods admitted, "but we are being very selective. Our strategy hasn't changed over the last year just because Bo's become even more famous. We want limited exposure, always keeping in mind that Bo's primary commitment is to his sport, in season." (In early 1990, Bo became a TV spokesman for AT&T.)

Bo picked up where he left off before the All-Star break, hitting a three-run homer and driving in five runs in a victory over Minnesota on July 18, but an injury to his left quadricep muscle eight days later sidelined him for two weeks. Though the injury slowed Jackson in August, Bo heated up when the AL West pennant race got hot at the start of September. On the first of the month, Bo's eighth-inning homer tied a game that the Royals eventually won against Texas in extra frames. The victory brought Kansas City to within one and a half games of the division-leading Oakland Athletics. But despite homers by Bo in four out of the next six games and three RBI's for a victory on September 9, the Royals never got any closer to first. They ended the season at 90–72 and in second place, seven games behind the eventual world-champion Athletics.

Even with Bo's second-half falloff, a slump that probably cost him a shot at the AL's Most Valuable Player award, his season was a raging success by any measure. His 32 home runs and 105 RBI's were fourth in the league and were both team-leading figures. He also led the Royals in slugging percentage (.495, sixth in the league), runs scored (86, tied for tenth in the league), and total bases (255). He stole 26 bases, making him a 25-homer, 25-steals man for the second straight year, and he led the league in RBI ratio, with one ribbie for every 4.9 at-bats. Bo also produced baseball's second-best run production average (.352; compiled by adding runs and RBI's and dividing by plate appearances), and was the American League's most dangerous road hitter (a league-leading 59 road ribbies and a .554 slugging average). Defensively, he cut down 11 base runners with his bullet outfield throws.

The only negative statistic on Bo's 1989 résumé was his strikeout totals. His 172 strikeouts led the AL and was a club record, but one baseball writer even managed to turn that stat into a positive one. *The New York Times*'s Murray Chass pointed out that though Jackson whiffed once out of every 2.99 times at bat, in his other 343 times to the plate he compiled a .385 "contact average." Jackson ranked third in the majors in this department among the 42 players who struck out 100 or more times. While that contact average statistic certainly is impressive, the Royals would probably prefer that if Bo has to make an out, he do it in ways that can advance a base runner or two.

Still, there was no doubt that in 1989 Bo Jackson established himself as one of baseball's brightest stars and one of its most impressive talents. In a poll of major-league managers conducted by *Baseball America,* Jackson was ranked as number one in the league in four categories: hitter with the best power; fastest base runner; outfielder with the best arm; and most exciting player. The poll results and Bo's season made Ken Gonzales proud.

"All those scouts during Bo's college years who said he would never make it in baseball, I wonder what they're saying now," Gonzales said. "But the more I watched him, the more I felt I was watching something that comes along once every fifty years or so. I don't know if I'll be alive the next time another Bo Jackson comes around, so I'd just like to enjoy this one as much as I can."

If anyone wants to know whether Bo now knows baseball superstardom, all he'd have to do is ask one of the men who evaluates major-leaguers for a living.

"I've been scouting this game for fifty years," longtime baseball bird dog Hugh Alexander said in *Baseball America,* "and so everybody asks me: 'Who're the best ballplayers I've ever seen?' I always tell them the same four: Babe Ruth, Joe DiMaggio, Willie Mays, and Roberto Clemente. I don't say Stan Musial or Hank Aaron because I learned that the really great ballplayers can beat you five different ways: throwing, running, fielding, hitting, and hitting home runs. Only the great ones can excel in all of those phases.

"Now, I tell you what. I may have to be adding another name to that list pretty doggone soon. His name is Bo Jackson."

A ballplayer can't receive a better tribute than that.

11

Who Knows Bo?

Great American athletes become famous for as many legendary off-the-field exploits as on-the-field feats. These are stories that possess the human-interest angles that sportswriters crave and that are woven into countless newspaper and magazine articles. If such tales were sports statistics, Bo Jackson would be a league leader.

There are stories that go all the way back to Bo's days at Auburn. One is reminiscent of those sappy scenes in sports movies—you know, the ones in which heroes give sick kids in hospitals the will to go on living. Seems a station wagon collided with a fourteen-year-old boy on a bicycle, necessitating the amputation of the kid's right leg. Angered and depressed, the boy refused to eat and his weight dropped to 90 pounds. The hospital dietician, who graduated from Auburn, discovered that the boy idolized Bo Jackson. She wrote to Bo asking for his autograph. Jackson did better than that. He called the boy and offered encouragement, sent him autographed pictures, then went to the hospital and spent hours cheering the kid up. "He knows I care," said Bo, and that effort may have saved a boy's life.

Another incident occurred one day when Bo was driving

from his Bessemer home to a summer job at a Birmingham
bank. A woman who had crashed into a guardrail on the
interstate lay stunned in her smoking auto. The car could
have exploded at any moment, but Jackson, who was driving by, stopped and quickly pulled the woman out. He
kept the story a secret for weeks. "I didn't feel it was that
important," Bo explained when he finally revealed the incident. "I was just doing what was right."

There's the story about Bo watching a television news
item about a junior-college basketball player whose feet
were so big—size 21—that he couldn't find basketball
shoes. Jackson called Nike and had the company send the
kid some custom-made sneakers. But Bo also told Nike
that he didn't want the story publicized.

Then there's the story about the time in early 1989 when
Bo was driving around Kansas City running errands and
happened upon an auto accident. Car after car sped by,
ignoring an injured man and his girlfriend. Bo stopped his
car, called paramedics, and stayed with the couple until an
ambulance arrived. The couple didn't know who it was
who had helped them. "I couldn't believe people drove
past them," Bo would say when relating the incident.
"The guy's head was all busted open. Even if it was my
worst enemy, I'd stop and help."

So Bo knows kindness, consideration, and good deeds.
He's obviously come a long way from those days when he
had one foot in a reform school. All these stories make
great copy for sportswriters, sure, but do they really capture the essence of the man? Hardly. Though Bo Jackson
has become one of America's most ubiquitous sports per-
sonalities, though we see him on playing fields practically
all year round and watch him on television selling Nikes
almost every day, Bo Jackson is a superstar America
doesn't really know. If this phenomenon has a talent for

anything, it's for keeping his on-field and off-field lives distinctly separate, protecting his privacy, and for fashioning an image as an enigma. Bo has readily admitted that "the idea is to never let the public know my next move."

Bo won't even give his home telephone number to the media relations departments of his respective teams, a strategy which helps keep an insistent press at bay. "The leverage I might have from playing two sports never takes a part in how I act," Jackson said in the April 1990 *GQ* magazine. "I wouldn't use it that way. If someone disrespects me, I lose respect for them. A lot of people can act the way I do, if they learn to stand up for what's right."

It is precisely such an attitude that has caused more than one sportswriter (especially before Jackson achieved his most recent glory) to suggest that Bo knows arrogance. Jackson doesn't go out of his way to discourage that perception.

For example, he could explain that his penchant for referring to himself in the third person is easier than stuttering his way through "I-I-I-I," yet he doesn't. He once said, "I'm not going to try to change what people think of me. I'm just going to be myself. I'm just going to be Bo."

For Bo, to change or even form a public image of himself would mean opening up to reporters, something he feels would intrude on his time and privacy. He has been known to dismiss sportswriters' questions with a glare. When he does talk to writers or attend press conferences, his face registers the uncomfortable look of someone who'd rather be someplace else. "I never even read the sports pages," Bo once admitted.

And when sports fans read about Jackson, they find out he has a passion for hunting and fishing, that in 1989 he bought a Ferrari Testarossa and started wearing a diamond earring in his left ear, that he has an intelligent, loving wife and two sons, that he has homes in Kansas City and Alabama and apartments in Southern California and Florida. But they find out little about what motivates Bo, what discourages Bo, what thrills Bo. The most philosophical comments one might read from him are statements like "My childhood made me a very determined man" or "I try to take things one day at a time—do just enough to keep everybody happy." These remarks don't tell us much. What's the only way to discover what makes Bo tick? Sift through the recorded material, piece it all together, and, like a Kremlinologist analyzing Soviet policy before the Cold War thaw, draw conclusions as to what it all means. Here's what we do know about the side of Bo that doesn't swing bats, carry footballs, or pitch products:

Bo and religion: Even many of Bo's closest friends don't know that he is a man with strong spiritual beliefs. On those infrequent occasions when Bo is quoted while philosophizing about sports and success, he will touch on the religious influences on his talent and career. "The joy I get in sport is from just competing," he told *Time* magazine in 1986. "I enjoy the sweet gifts of body and mind that thousands wish they had. The Lord is watching every move I make and making extra sure that I'm not misusing my talents. And in 1989, Bo revealed to *The Sporting News:* "When it comes to sports and religion, the public and press have got their priorities mixed up. Instead of asking a person how they feel about the game spiritually, or how does the Lord help you get here, they're asking about everything else.

"I'll tell everyone who asks that I'm blessed. The athletic skill I have is not because Bo Jackson was born with it, but because the Lord gave it to me."

Bo and his teammates: Besides proving that he was a

major-league-caliber player, one of Jackson's major challenges when he first joined the Kansas City Royals was to earn the respect of fellow players. He'd made a bad first impression after his signing in 1986, when he left autographed pictures of himself with the Heisman Trophy in the Royals locker room. And the relationship wasn't helped any when he decided to play football in 1987. Slowly but surely, though, he won them over with his talent, his exuberance, and his leadership. Resentment was transformed into reverence.

After a 1988 game in Milwaukee, Royals outfielder Willie Wilson and his fiancée were verbally abused by some fans hurling racial insults. When it looked as though Wilson might be attacked, he appealed to some teammates, including Bo, for help. Nasty words were exchanged, sleeves were being rolled up, and a fight appeared ready to break out. Then the hecklers saw the hulking presence of Bo Jackson and backed off faster than Bo runs the bases.

"Bo doesn't like to be the center of attention," said Wilson, who had been one of Bo's biggest critics, "but when it comes down to helping people, he's softhearted. People don't realize what a good person he is, but he's one of the finest persons I've ever known."

Royals pitcher Tom Gordon would agree with that sentiment. Gordon made the team as a rookie in 1989, but didn't have his own place in Kansas City. Jackson let the young player move in with his family until Gordon found his own place. "Bo's helped me out like I was his kid," Gordon said.

On the field, the Royals were impressed with the intensity of Bo's team-oriented attitude. They found that Bo treated almost every game as if it were a football war. "Bo is really naïve in terms of baseball, because he really is into that Joe College, rah-rah stuff," Royals Bill Buckner told

Sports Illustrated in 1989. "We kid him about it, but he's very serious about it. He thinks every day is Auburn-Alabama."

Bo's agent, Richard Woods, likes to relate how when his client calls during the baseball season to report about a victory, he doesn't talk about his role in the win. "The next morning," Woods said, "I find out in the box score that he got three hits."

Jackson's philosophy of team play is simple: "I'm not the kind of person that will go out and do things self-ishly," he said on a Birmingham television special called "Bo Jackson: The Making of a Legend." "I try to look out for my teammates more than myself because on the field of play I try to be a leader. You can't have a tribe and not have a chief, so I try to be the guy with the feather in his hat when I'm out there."

Bo and children: Jackson is a spokesperson for the President's Council on Physical Fitness. He is also affiliated with various hospitals in Alabama and Kansas City, including KC's Marillac Cancer Center, which works with child cancer patients (Bo gave the center the van he won as the 1989 All-Star Game MVP). He's filmed anti-drug spots for television, and for every home run he hits, he donates $500 (which the Royals match) to a Kansas City charity for disturbed children. But Bo's concern for children, whether sick or healthy, didn't just begin when he became a star and felt obligated to connect with a charity. It has its roots back at Auburn, when Bo became a child-development major. Part of the curriculum involved visiting centers for troubled children, where Bo would talk about right and wrong and the evils of drugs. "Don't get mixed up with the bad stuff the way I did," he would tell youngsters, "or you'll end up in the penitentiary before you're twenty-one, which is where I was headed."

"He was very sincere," one of the center's faculty said. "He had a real concern for children as people. He made it a point to get down to their eye level to talk to them. He sat with them. He didn't stand up and lecture. And because he was famous, they listened."

And during an era when baseball players can make thousands an hour at card shows just by sitting at a desk and scribbling their names, Jackson's autograph can be had for free. "Bo has turned down the most lucrative offer he's had, doing these paid-autograph signing parties," revealed Richard Woods. "But Bo says he won't make a kid pay for an autograph. I've seen him stand three hours signing autographs after a game."

Bo and the fans: Jackson won't sign any autographs, however, if it means taking "private, quality time" away from his family. "Fans want to get as close as possible to athletes," Bo told *USA Today.* "What they fail to realize is that there are times and places for all that. I think I belong to the public at the ball park. It's not like I wear that uniform twenty-four hours a day."

Once Jackson leaves the baseball or football stadium—what he refers to as "punching out"—he wants to be as private and inconspicuous as possible. He doesn't want to be bothered by what he calls, "the outside world." In *GQ* magazine he revealed that. "Before my wife and I go to dinner, I tell her that if anybody comes up to the table, asks me to sign a napkin, I'm going to cuss them out. She says, 'Don't you dare,' I have to smile sweetly and say, 'I have to do that at the ballpark.' What I'd like to tell them is where to take that napkin and shove it."

Bo and family: Away from the ball park, Bo easily assumes the role of father and husband. He comes home after games feeling completely exhausted, but is never too tired to play with his sons, four-year-old Garrett and two-year-old Nicholas. "The job he's done with his children is a beautiful thing," Hal Baird once observed. "He takes more pride in being a father than he does in being an athlete."

Bo's wife, Linda, likes to tell a story about how when Nicholas was delivered in August of 1988, Jackson wouldn't let go of his new son until the nurse practically pulled the baby out of his hands. "I fell in love with him all over again," Linda said. "It was such an emotional moment. He was holding Nicholas and crying. I could see the look on the nurse's face. She was shocked that this was Bo Jackson, that he was so human and so nice."

Ultimately, nobody knows Bo as well as Linda, who postponed her doctoral studies in counseling psychology to raise the children and support her husband's career. ("He's not going to play ball but a few years," she has said. "I can be a therapist my whole life.") Since she met him at Auburn, Linda has observed Bo's attempts to keep his distance from people who may try take advantage of him.

"We're almost opposites," Linda related to the *Kansas City Star*. "Bo is much more reserved and less talkative. Because he has stuttered since he was a child, and because he doesn't say much to people he doesn't know, people assume he's not that smart. But he's a lot smarter than people give him credit for. He's open with people he feels real comfortable with. On some level, I think, he's a bit shy. If you were a fly on the wall and saw him around here with me and the kids, you wouldn't recognize him."

Bo and the future: When Jackson left Auburn in 1986, he was 23 credits short of his degree in family-and-child development. But he was determined to carry out that promise he'd made to his mother about being the first in the family to earn a degree. So between the end of the

1989 football season and the start of 1990 spring baseball training, he resumed his studies at Auburn. It appears that Bo Jackson's future doesn't only include breaking sports records, winning awards, and making millions. It also includes, among other things, helping children. After he left Auburn in 1986, he talked about one day building a multi-purpose day-care center "where mothers who work could leave their babies, troubled teen-agers into drugs could go for help, and it would be a place that would be a retirement home for older folks." In the past few years, he talked about establishing a counseling practice with Linda. "She would be the boss," he insisted, before joking, "but I think she would hire me."

Bo Jackson has already earned his degree in baseball, football, and family. Now he's going after his Ph.D. as a human being.

BO JACKSON'S PROFESSIONAL STATISTICS

BASEBALL

YEAR	CLUB	AVG.	G	AB	R	H	2B	3B	HR	RBI	BB	SO	SB
1986	Memphis	.277	53	184	30	51	9	3	7	25	22	81	3
	K.C. Royals	.207	25	82	9	17	2	1	2	9	7	34	3
1987	K.C. Royals	.235	116	396	46	93	17	2	22*	53	30	158	10
1988	K.C. Royals	.246	124	439	63	108	16	4	25	68	25	146	27
1989	K.C. Royals	.256	135	515	86	132	15	6	32	105	39	172	26
M.L. TOTALS		.244	400	1432	204	350	50	13	81	235	101	510	66

FOOTBALL

YEAR	CLUB	ATTEMPTS	YARDS	AVG	TDs	Lg.
1987	L.A. Raiders	81	554	6.8	4	91
1988	L.A. Raiders	136	580	4.3	3	25
1989	L.A. Raiders	173	950	5.5	4	92
NFL TOTALS		390	2084	5.3	11	92

*CLUB RECORD

BO JACKSON'S COLLEGIATE STATISTICS

FOOTBALL—CAREER RUSHING (NOT INCLUDING BOWL GAMES)

YEAR	CLUB	GAMES	ATT	YARDS	AVG.	TDs	LG.	AVG/G	100-TD.	200-YD.
1982	AUBURN	11	127	829	6.5	9	53	75.4	5	0
1983	AUBURN	11	158	1213	7.7	12	80	110.3	5	1
1984	AUBURN	6	87	475	5.5	5	53	79.2	2	0
1985	AUBURN	11	278	1786*	6.4	17*	76	162.4	8*	4
TOTALS		38	650	4303*	6.7*	43*	80	113.2*	21*	5*

FOOTBALL—CAREER RECEIVING

YEAR	CLUB	NUMBER	YARDS	AVG.	TD	LG
1982	AUBURN	5	64	12.8	0	43
1983	AUBURN	13	73	5.6	2	44
1984	AUBURN	4	62	15.5	0	21
1985	AUBURN	4	73	18.3	0	29
TOTALS		26	272	10.5	2	44

*AUBURN RECORD

1985 Heisman Memorial Trophy Balloting

Name	College	Total Votes			Total
		1st	2nd	3rd	Points
1. Bo Jackson	Auburn University	317	218	122	1,509
2. Chuck Long	University of Iowa	286	254	98	1,464
3. Robbie Bosco	Brigham Young Univ.	38	95	155	459
4. Lorenzo White	Michigan State Univ.	50	63	115	391
5. Vinny Testaverde	University of Miami	41	41	44	249
6. Jim Everett	Purdue University	12	11	19	77
7. Napoleon McCallum	United States Naval Academy	8	11	26	72
8. Allen Pinkett	University of Notre Dame	9	13	18	71
9. Joe Dudek	Plymouth State College	12	4	12	56
10. Brian McClure	Bowling Green St. Univ.	7	10	13	54
Thurman Thomas	Oklahoma State Univ.	1	13	25	54

BO! IN THE AUBURN FOOTBALL RECORD BOOK

Career Rushing: 1st with 4,303 yards
    James Brooks is 2nd with 3,523; Joe Cribbs is 3rd with 3,368.
Season Rushing: 1st with 1786 in 1985
    James Brooks is 2nd with 1,314 in 1980.
Rushing Yards in a Game: 2nd behind Curtis Kuykendall (307 vs. Miami in 1944)
    Bo had 290 vs. SW Louisiana in 1985.
Rushing Yards in an SEC Game: 1st with 256 yards vs. Alabama in 1983
Rushing Yards Gained Per Game, Career: 1st with 113.2 in 38 games
    92.7 by James Brooks is 2nd.
Average Per Carry, Season: 2nd behind Tommy Lorino (8.6 in 1956)
    Bo averaged 7.7 per carry in 1983 and averaged 6.7 yards in 1985.
Average Per Carry, Career: 1st with 6.7 -per-carry average
    6.03 by Fob James is 2nd.
100-Yard Games, Season: 1st with 8 in 1985
    Joe Cribbs is 2nd with 7 in 1978.
100-Yard Games, Career: 1st with 21
    James Brooks is 2nd with 15.
Consecutive 100-Yard Games, Season: 2nd behind James Brooks's 5 in 1980
    Bo had a 4-game streak in 1985; he had 4 straight in 1983.
200-Yard Games, Career: 1st with 5 (4 in 1985 and 1 in 1983)
    James Brooks is 2nd with 4.

BO JACKSON

Consecutive 200-Yard Games: tied for 1st with 2 ; 295 vs. SW La. and 205 vs. So. Miss. in 1985; James Brooks had 204 vs. Richmond and 210 vs. LSU in 1980.

Rushing Touchdowns, Season: 1st with 17 in 1985
   Joe Cribbs is 2nd with 16 in 1978.

Touchdowns Scored, Career: 1st with 44 (43 rushing and 1 receiving)
   Joe Cribbs is 2nd with 34.

Points Scored, Career: 1st with 274
   Al Del Greco (PK) is 2nd with 236.

Points Scored, Season: 1st with 102 in 1985
   Joe Cribbs is 2nd with 96 in 1978.
   Bo had 90 in 1985.

BASEBALL—CAREER

YEAR	CLUB	GAMES	AVG.	AB	R	H	HR	RBI	BB	SO	SB
1983	Auburn	26	.279	68	14	19	4	13	20	34	5
1984	Auburn			Did Not Play—Ran Track							
1985	Auburn	42	.401	147	55	59	17	43	26	41	9
1986	Auburn	*21	.246	69	21	17	7	14	20	30	5
TOTALS		89	.335	284	90	95	28	70	66	105	19

*Played Last game 3-24-86—Suspended for NCAA violation

Stephen Hanks is a writer and editor who has co-published national magazines on baseball and football. His magazine articles have appeared in *Esquire; Memories, The Village Voice, Inside Sports,* and *Sport Magazine,* and he recently authored *The Game That Changed Pro Football,* a book about the New York Jets' Super Bowl III upset of the Baltimore Colts in 1969. His most recent book for St. Martin's Paperbacks was a biography of hockey superstar Wayne Gretzky. Hanks lives in Brooklyn, New York.